# QUEENS
## OF THE TURF

Edited by Andrew Pennington
Foreword by Lester Piggott

**RACING POST**

# Contents

## The Queens

# Foreword
## Lester Piggott

During my riding career I rode – or rode against – several of the 50 mares and fillies whose careers are described in these pages. But there are three which will always have a special place in my memories: Petite Etoile, Park Top and Dahlia.

Petite Etoile was undoubtedly the greatest of her sex that I ever rode, which makes it all the more remarkable that she showed us very little as a two-year-old in 1958. So little that I did not ride her in the 1959 1,000 Guineas, preferring her stable companion Collyria. Doug Smith came in for a nice spare ride on Petite Etoile, and you can imagine how I felt watching him cruise home on the iron-grey filly. I did not make the same mistake again, riding her to easy wins in the Oaks, Sussex Stakes, Yorkshire Oaks and Champion Stakes. As a four-year-old in 1960 she landed the Coronation Cup before being narrowly beaten by Aggressor in the King George VI and Queen Elizabeth Stakes at Ascot, and she rewarded the decision to keep her in training as a five-year-old in 1961 by winning a second Coronation Cup, though in my opinion she had lost the brilliance she had shown at three and four.

On Park Top I won the Coronation Cup and King George among many other top races, and at her best she was almost as good as Petite Etoile. But she had more than her fair share of bad luck, and one unusual memory of this fine mare was her owner the Duke of Devonshire giving the old-fashioned V-sign to Longchamp racegoers who had booed her after we had been beaten in the Prix Royallieu.

Then there was Dahlia. She was one of the toughest and most professional horses I ever rode – male or female – but she was highly strung, and could get quite mulish before a race. We scarcely came out of a canter to win her second King George in 1974, after which she registered the first of her two victories in the Benson and Hedges Gold Cup at York. The same year we won the prestigious Woodbine International in Toronto. Quite simply, Dahlia was a tremendous racehorse.

Three undisputed champions, but I must mention one other filly who does not feature in this book but has a special place in my memories: Carrozza, who won the Oaks by a short head in 1957, the only Classic winner I rode in the colours of Her Majesty the Queen.

This book is a wonderful way of celebrating the fillies and mares who have illuminated racing over the centuries – truly, the Queens of the Turf.

**TOUGHNESS PERSONIFIED: I return on Dahlia after the second of our two victories in the Benson and Hedges Gold Cup at York in August 1975**

# Introduction
## Bruce Millington

**Racing Post editor**

A great racehorse is a great racehorse, but there's something even more special about a great filly or mare, and each of our racing lives has been enhanced by the careers of some phenomenal equine females.

In my teenage years my crushes were not just on singers and actresses, but fantastic horses like Pebbles, Time Charter, Soba and Dawn Run, who cemented my love for racing.

They have been followed down the years by many other superb fillies and mares, and it was on a drive to Cheltenham in the autumn of 2016 that it occurred to me there might be some interest among *Racing Post* readers in a list of the best female racers of all time.

I put out a hopeful tweet to gauge interest and was astonished by the response. Literally hundreds of people replied within an hour naming their favourite fillies and mares, and it was instantly clear we had something big on our hands.

With the help of features editor Katherine Fidler we set about creating a top 50, no easy task given how many flying fillies have graced the courses down the centuries.

We quickly agreed this would be a celebration of the best female talent throughout history rather than a handicapping exercise that would require painstaking form assessments to decide the precise placings of the final countdown.

And we had to make decisions about the Flat/jumps split and how deep we would go into the annals of history to ensure we captured the greats of generations past.

With the help of various *Racing Post* experts we managed to finalise what we hope is a credible top 50, and given the marvellous materials we were working with I can safely say is has been one of the most enjoyable tasks of my career.

A personal favourite if I may: Pebbles's victory in the 1985 Champion Stakes was as exhilarating a sporting moment as I can remember. Pat Eddery's leisurely look to his right as he swept into the lead aboard Sheikh Mohammed's aeroplane of a filly is one of my all-time favourite racing moments.

Hopefully this book contains some of your favourite sporting memories too. Hopefully, too, you will enjoy reliving the majesty of these brilliant fillies and mares as much as we have enjoyed recreating their stories.

> "Pebbles's victory in the 1985 Champion Stakes was as exhilarating a sporting moment as I can remember"

# 01
# PRETTY POLLY

By the end of 1902, devotees of the British turf were marvelling at the three-year-old season of one of the finest horses the sport had ever seen, and no doubt wondering if they would ever see her like again. Surely such excellence as was being shown by four-time Classic winner Sceptre would not be repeated for generations to come; and if another shining star had already been born, then pedigree suggested it could not be the two-year-old Pretty Polly, no matter how impressive a juvenile haul she amassed.

Pretty Polly was a daughter of the Irish-based stallion Gallinule, who for all his success at stud had the dubious distinction of being both a 'bleeder' and a 'roarer' – a breaker of blood vessels who made a fearful commotion when breathing. Her mother was Admiration, a chestnut broodmare bought by Major Eustace Loder for his Eyrefield Lodge Stud near the Curragh, whose undistinguished legs were matched only by her uninspiring pedigree and decidedly patchy racing career, which took in two minor Flat wins in Ireland and ended in a military steeplechase.

Compared to the noble Sceptre, the white-starred chestnut was racing riff-raff, yet by the time she had finished her first season on the track in 1903, in the care of Peter Gilpin in Newmarket, Pretty Polly had channelled the fiery spirit that saw her get into several scrapes in her early days of training, and won nine races of increasing status (including the Champagne, Cheveley Park and Middle Park Stakes) from nine juvenile starts, often in little more than a hack canter.

Far from being a mere foil for the continued supremacy of Sceptre, in defeating the best colts of her generation, including subsequent 2,000 Guineas and Derby winner St Amant, she announced herself as a worthy rival for the blueblood filly. That they never met on the track, despite two years of common ground, remains a source of regret, although they did win races at Newmarket just half an hour apart in Pretty Polly's first campaign.

As the season progressed, the idiosyncratic filly developed a liking for both regular young rider William Lane and her constant companion, the cute little cob Little Missus, who often went with her to the start and accompanied her back to the stables. Pretty Polly also came to expect a sugar lump as a reward in the winner's enclosure, to be administered by the trainer's wife. Her quirks made her a crowd favourite.

The crack juvenile sprinter still had much work to do if she were to convince the cognoscenti she was a match for Sceptre. Reckoned by many to be too quick to stay even a mile, she nonetheless justified strong favouritism to win both the Guineas and Oaks on a tight rein – at Epsom receiving her sugar lump treat from no less a celebrity than King Edward VII – and followed up in the Coronation and Nassau Stakes.

Given that she beat St Amant pointless once again in the St Leger, it was a cause of lasting regret to connections that she hadn't been entered in the colts' Classic at Epsom, but she pressed on regardless, taking the Park Hill just two days after the Leger, in so doing racking up her 15th straight win and completing a double that had proved beyond even Sceptre.

Undone by a rough crossing, heavy ground, unfavourable weights and the absence of her injured friend Lane, she was beaten at Longchamp on her next run under Danny Maher. Lane would never ride her again, but that proved no long-term barrier to her dominance.

She won her final start of the season under Maher in Newmarket's Free Handicap and as a four-year-old took up where she left off, shrugging off an injury that kept her out of the Ascot Gold Cup, landing the first of two Coronation Cup successes, under Herbert Madden in the yellow, with dark blue sleeves, before scoring bloodless victories in the Champion Stakes, Limekiln Stakes (at 55-1 on) and 2m2f Jockey Club Cup (ridden by Gilpin's stable jockey Bernard Dillon), giving the lie to Maher's oft-voiced assertion that she was a non-stayer.

The tally was up to 20 wins by now, with the 21st coming in the March Stakes the following spring on her final visit to the Rowley Mile, the 22nd at Epsom

**Foaled**
1901
**Pedigree**
Gallinule – Admiration
**Breeder**
Major Eustace Loder
**Owner**
Major Eustace Loder
**Trainer**
Peter Gilpin
**Main jockey**
William Lane
**Career record**
22 wins and two places from 24 runs
**Most famous for**
Her fillies' Triple Crown, among 22 victories from sprint trips to extreme distances, in an illustrious four-year career. Named Broodmare of the Century in the book *A Century of Champions* by John Randall and Tony Morris

"By the time she had finished her first season on the track, Pretty Polly had channelled the fiery spirit that saw her get into several scrapes in her early days of training"

for her second Coronation Cup. It was to prove her final moment of glory on the track.

One contemporary observer reported that "a silence as of death" greeted Pretty Polly's one-length defeat by Bachelor's Button and Maher in the Ascot Gold Cup of 1906 – perhaps undone by any combination of a troublesome wart, steamy weather conditions and the absence of Little Missus, but beaten nonetheless. It would have been less of a tragedy had she not jarred herself in training in the lead-up to the Doncaster Cup, robbing her of the chance to end her career on a victorious note.

She was retired to Loder's stud in the October of that year, departing the scene with a reputation that exceeded even that of Sceptre, only twice defeated in 24 starts, victorious from five furlongs to 2m2f. Robert Sievier, owner and trainer of Sceptre, declared the pair "both too good to be compared".

At Stud, Pretty Polly proved an initial disappointment, yet went on to found great dynasties. Her six colt foals were underwhelming, but her four fillies,

despite mixed results on the track, all returned to Eyrefield to establish important branches in the Stud Book that resonate even now, her matriarchal influence extending to the likes of St Paddy and Brigadier Gerard.

Of those daughters, Molly Desmond produced five winners, including dual Irish Classic heroes Zodiac and Spike Island, and the key broodmares Lady Maureen, Molly Adare and Sarita; Dutch Mary bred six significant winners, including St James's Palace winner Christopher Robin; Polly Flinders gave birth to Arabella, whose granddaughter Overture bred 12 winners in a line that extends in the modern era to Marwell, Unite and Paean; Baby Polly was the mother of Doncaster Cup winner Colorado Kid and was third dam of Vienna, the sire of Vaguely Noble.

Pretty Polly, who had top-class races named after her in England and Ireland, was put down at the age of 30 and buried at Eyrefield – a true Queen of the Turf, never to be forgotten.
PETER THOMAS

PEERLESS PERFORMER: Pretty Polly, pictured with jockey Bernard Dillon, raced for four years and was beaten just twice in 24 starts

# 02

# PEBBLES

Aqueduct Park, 1985. "England's superfilly Pebbles has won it" came the call as the chestnut filly with the striking white blaze galloped into the pantheons of the turf on her final start. Under a balls-of-steel ride from Pat Eddery, Pebbles lit up New York, her relentless turn of foot sending her up the inside and into the record books as the first British-trained winner at the Breeders' Cup.

Yet like so many to have featured in this comprehensive list of the sport's finest females, that majestic moment which defined a career was in stark contrast to the undulating journey that had taken her there.

"She was a character," said Clive Brittain, the man who masterminded her rise and who quickly established this combustible filly needed a calming influence.

Step forward gelded Royal Hunt Cup winner Come On The Blues, who relaxed his stablemate both at home, where their adjoining stables shared an open window, and when accompanying her to the races.

Not trained in the conventional way either, she would spend more time in the pool than on the gallops and was a big fan of Guinness, a tipple many of Brittain's finest horses consumed to "sharpen the appetite".

Her career began inconspicuously, finishing down the field in a Sandown maiden as an unconsidered 33-1 shot, but victories followed at Newbury and Newmarket before her first real test in the Lowther at York.

She started fourth in the betting and, far from disgraced, filled the same position behind three previous winners. She went backwards on her next run, however, the occasion seemingly getting the better of her in a Group 3 at Goodwood. Failing to settle, she was spent in the closing stages and managed only fifth.

Happy to back his own judgement, Brittain was never shy to test Group 1 waters but plans to run Pebbles in the Cheveley Park Stakes looked ambitious even by his standards.

**"Only a shake of the rein was required for her to effortlessly open up three lengths on a champion. It was poetry in motion"**

**BLAZE OF GLORY: Pebbles and Philip Robinson are led in by the filly's then owner Captain Marcos Lemos after winning the 1,000 Guineas at Newmarket in 1984**

Her price reflected her form and she was once again sent off at 33-1, yet putting in her best work in the final furlong, she split Desirable and Prickle – both of whom had beaten her emphatically at York – in a photo-finish. Unsurprised, Brittain was convinced he was dealing with something out of the ordinary.

"I've been so lucky to have great fillies like User Friendly, Sayyedati and Crimplene, but she was unique – she was a class above everything else," said her trainer.

Pebbles, not one who stood out in a crowd, was a cosy winner of the Nell Gwyn on her reappearance the following season but, thanks to the presence of Fred Darling heroine and hot favourite Mahogany, was overlooked when lining up for the 1,000 Guineas.

While the market leader impressed in the pre-lims, Pebbles was edgy, sweating badly and even lucky to make it to the start in one piece.

"As she was coming out onto the course, she suddenly spun right round hitting a gate – it was a worrying moment," jockey Philip Robinson later revealed.

Unscathed, she was keen in the early stages of the race but a strong pace helped her settle in a prominent position. Then came the decisive move. Angled to the far rail she quickened on demand, striding clear for a convincing win and handing her rider a first Classic.

Owned and bred by Greek shipping magnate Captain Marcos Lemos, Pebbles was the first foal of La Dolce, who had finished fifth in the 1979 Oaks and connections set about teaching her daughter to settle with her own Epsom bid in mind.

However, a fortnight before the mile-and-a-half Classic came an enforced change of plan. Lemos sold Pebbles to Sheikh Mohammed, who already had two fancied Oaks contenders and it was decided to send her for the Coronation Stakes instead.

It failed to pay off, with Brittain pointing to the fact her training had been geared towards a step up in trip after her length-and-a-half defeat by Irish Guineas heroine Katies, a brilliant filly herself.

A rematch was scheduled for Newmarket's July meeting, only for a chip in a near-fore to sideline Pebbles until the autumn. She would instead reappear in the Champion Stakes, which provided a first test against her elders, and a first try beyond a mile.

Ridden from well off the pace, she swept through the field, only failing by a neck to overhaul French raider Palace Music. It was a career best that prompted connections to keep her in training for what proved a defining four-year-old season.

**Foaled**
February 27, 1981
**Pedigree**
Sharpen Up – La Dolce
**Breeder**
Marcos Lemos
**Owner**
Sheikh Mohammed
**Trainer**
Clive Brittain
**Main jockeys**
Pat Eddery and
Steve Cauthen
**Career record**
Eight wins and four places from 15 runs
**Most famous for**
A Classic winner at three and champion at four. Her wins in the Eclipse, Champion Stakes and Breeders' Cup Turf being the highlights

**Fate at stud**
Despite producing foals by prominent stallions like Nureyev, Caerleon, Green Desert and Reference Point, none of her progeny distinguished themselves as racehorses. In 1996 Pebbles was sent to Darley Japan, where she retired from breeding in 2002. She died in 2005 at the age of 24

Her third and final campaign began with an easy win over a mile in a Group 2 at Sandown, but she was again defeated at Royal Ascot, this time in the Prince of Wales's Stakes behind 33-1 shot Bob Back, although was later found to have been in season.

Next came the Eclipse, a race with a 99-year history but without a filly on its roll of honour. With Coronation Cup hero Rainbow Quest at odds-on, it seemed unlikely Pebbles was destined to be the first.

Yet overcoming the odds when it seemed most unlikely was becoming her hallmark and, in a tactical race, she readily outpointed Rainbow Quest by two lengths.

The King George at Ascot was the natural next step, but just as it seemed Pebbles was conquering her quirks and fulfilling her true potential, she inexplicably lost her appetite. Off her feed for two months no less, Brittain's patience was tested to the limit as she threatened to waste away.

Perhaps thanks to Guinness, her hunger eventually returned and onlookers were surprised to see her looking so well as she returned for a vintage Champion Stakes at Newmarket.

Hyped as a clash between runaway Derby hero Slip Anchor and the previous year's St Leger winner Commanche Run, Pebbles left them for dead with a performance that has to be seen to be believed – check it out on YouTube.

Settled way off the pace by Eddery, she glided along the stands' rail and was simply cantering as she joined Slip Anchor in front rank. Only a shake of the rein was required for her to effortlessly open up three lengths on a champion who had won the Derby by seven. It was poetry in motion.

"She made them look like platers," said Brittain. "What she showed that day was her amazing speed, and that was her secret – her cantering speed was the same as most when they're flat out."

Arriving in America with Come On The Blues and a keg of stout for one last hurrah in the Breeders' Cup Turf, Pebbles overcame a stinking draw in 14 under a daring ride from Eddery, scooting along the rail to trump Australian champion Strawberry Road by a neck and seal her place among the all-time greats.

"Her Breeders' Cup victory must be among the greatest days of my career," said Brittain, who bribed the gateman to let her in through the tradesmen's entrance at Aqueduct so she could miss the pre-race parade. "It would have blown her brain, so it was well worth a hundred bucks."

For a filly who was priceless, it certainly was.
**LEWIS PORTEOUS**

IN THE CLEAR: Pebbles becomes the first filly to win the Coral-Eclipse at Sandown in 1985 under Steve Cauthen

STAR PERFORMER: Pebbles canters to post under Pat Eddery before a scintillating victory in the 1985 Champion Stakes at Newmarket

# 03

# DAWN RUN

By virtue of being the only racehorse to win the Champion Hurdle and the Cheltenham Gold Cup, Dawn Run deserves an unchallenged status as the outstanding mare in the history of jump racing in Britain and Ireland. She also enjoys unique distinction as the winner of the hurdling championships in Britain, Ireland and France.

This supremacy was cloaked in drama, a narrative veering from the improbable Hollywood-style of an unforgettable Gold Cup to a fatal conclusion with echoes of a Greek tragedy. In among these were hints of the Shakespearean in the interplay between trainer Paddy Mullins, his jockey son Tony, and the mare's owner Charmian Hill, whose frail appearance and diminutive stature disguised a powerful personality and an iron force of will.

Dawn Run's significance in racing history extends beyond her feats at Cheltenham which, for all its accumulated tradition and prestige, is a relatively modern affair – the Gold Cup instituted in 1924, three years ahead of the inaugural Champion Hurdle. The mare, with Tony Mullins in the saddle, entered another historic realm on April 23, 1986 at Punchestown. Her match with Buck House, in which she dropped sharply in trip to defeat the Queen Mother Champion Chase winner at two miles and without the benefit of a sex allowance, places her in the great tradition which lies at the heart of steeplechasing. This late-20th century duel echoed the sport's origins in the match between Edmund Blake's runner and Cornelius O'Callaghan's representative that took place in County Cork in 1752, from the steeple of Buttevant Church to the spire of St Leger Church.

The previous month Dawn Run had completed the unprecedented Cheltenham double amid

scenes of unconfined joy. Embellished by Peter O'Sullevan's momentous observation – "and the mare is beginning to get up" – Dawn Run's effort from the last fence involved immense tenacity, a rallying surge, initially raising the prospect of gallant defeat, shifting almost imperceptibly towards the inexorable as she responded to Jonjo O'Neill's inspired riding to master the vastly experienced three-time King George winner Wayward Lad.

Dawn Run reached the summit that day, her coronation as the queen of jump racing. She was eight years old and had raced only five times over fences. The match at Punchestown was akin to a post-coronation parade.

Now Hill was keen to return to France where the mare had starred two seasons previously. Defeat in the Prix la Barka, a race she won in 1984, left Paddy Mullins thinking he should abandon the planned bid for a second win in the Grande Course de Haies. However, the owner prevailed, with disastrous consequences. Ridden by local jockey Michel Chirol, Dawn Run took a crashing fall at the fifth-last and suffered a broken neck. She had outlived Buck House, a victim of colic at home in Tipperary, by a matter of weeks.

There are several perspectives from which one can examine the mare's career. In terms of human drama, an intriguing sub-plot was provided by the fraught relationship between the Mullins family and Hill. However, this is not an appropriate place to delve into the specific details of a distant controversy. The purpose is rather to celebrate Dawn Run's achievements and qualities. As for the rest, there is no shortage of material in the public domain. The saga was detailed by writers Peter O'Neill and Sean Boyne in their 1995 biography of the great trainer Paddy Mullins, *The Master of Doninga*, which draws extensively on interviews with Paddy and Tony Mullins.

Born in 1918, Dawn Run's owner was a keen and capable horsewoman, a latecomer to race-riding when the Irish authorities belatedly granted women the right to compete against the men in 1974. She relished the challenge and achieved several wins

**Foaled**
April 27, 1978
**Pedigree**
Deep Run –
Twilight Slave
**Breeder**
John Riordan
**Owner**
Charmian Hill
**Trainer**
Paddy Mullins
**Main jockeys**
Tony Mullins and
Jonjo O'Neill
**Career record**
21 wins from 35 runs,
including one on the Flat
**Most famous for**
Completing the
Champion Hurdle/
Cheltenham Gold Cup
double, winning the
Champion Hurdle in
three countries

**"Dawn Run's peerless feats marked the pinnacle for Mullins and her Gold Cup victory was the crowning moment of O'Neill's career"**

on her horse Yes Man, trained by Mullins, including in a novice chase at Clonmel in 1979 a couple of months after her 61st birthday.

She was hospitalised for four months after Yes Man was killed in a fall at Clonmel in November 1980. Undeterred, she was not to be denied the opportunity to ride the 1978-foaled Deep Run filly out of Twilight Slave, whom she had bought at Ballsbridge for 5,800gns as an unbroken three-year-old. She rode Dawn Run to finish eighth on her debut in a bumper at Clonmel in May 1982. The following month the pair finished fourth at Thurles. Five days later her faith was vindicated with victory at Tralee.

Dawn Run was not spared during her novice hurdling campaign in the 1982–83 season. After an introduction under Peter Kavanagh at Naas in late November, she was ridden in her next five races by Tony Mullins, winning three. However, in the run-up to Cheltenham, Hill insisted on a change of jockey and Ron Barry was aboard when the mare finished second to the Martin Pipe-trained Sabin Du Loir in the Sun Alliance Hurdle. Mullins was re-instated at Aintree where she ran on consecutive days, winning the Page Three Hurdle, before losing out to the Champion Hurdle winner Gaye Brief in the Templegate Hurdle. She signed off with victory in the BMW Champion Novice Hurdle at Punchestown.

Tony Mullins rode the mare to win at Down Royal on her first start of the 1983–84 season before being replaced by O'Neill for the VAT Watkins Hurdle at Ascot. The mare suffered a reverse at Naas in December but redeemed herself with victory in the Christmas Hurdle at Kempton. She won the Wessel Cable Champion Hurdle at Leopardstown

**JOYOUS SCENES:**
Dawn Run and Jonjo O'Neill are led into the winner's enclosure after making history in the 1986 Cheltenham Gold Cup

in February before capturing the 1984 Champion Hurdle in her trademark aggressive style. Her immediate victim, 66-1 chance Cima, was a better horse than he was given credit for. Those behind included embryonic chasing stars Very Promising, Buck House and the great Desert Orchid.

On account of an injury to O'Neill, Tony Mullins was back to guide the mare to revenge over Gaye Brief in the Aintree Sandeman Hurdle. Kept on the go, she journeyed to Auteuil to win the Prix la Barka at the end of May. The following month she returned to the Paris track, stepping up in trip to win the Grande Course de Haies, the first Irish-trained winner since the pioneering Henry Linde sent out the subsequent Grand National winner Seaman in 1881.

The trainer's son rode Dawn Run to four of her five wins over fences, starting with a novice success at Navan in November 1984. The mare picked up an injury and was off for 13 months, resuming with victory in the Durkan Brothers Chase at Punchestown in December 1985. After beating Buck House in the Sean Graham Chase at Leopardstown the Gold Cup beckoned. In view of her relative inexperience it was decided she should get a taste of the Cheltenham fences in the Holsten Distributors Chase in January. She dominated the race from the front when hitting the final ditch hard, catapulting Mullins out of the saddle. The rider clung onto the reins and remounted, but must have guessed even then the inevitability of his fate. He would watch the mare's greatest triumph from the grandstand, as O'Neill and Dawn Run were practically carried into the winner's enclosure by a jubilant crowd.

The deaths of Buck House and Dawn Run came to exemplify a turning point in the fortunes of Irish jump racing, damaged by economic recession and the resultant drain of the best young jumping talent to Britain. There followed a period in which the Irish experience of the Cheltenham Festival was deeply depressing. Gradually a resurgence set in, but there was a ten-year hiatus between Dawn Run's Gold Cup win and Imperial Call's victory in 1996. It was another two years before Istabraq bridged the gap to the mare's Champion Hurdle win.

Dawn Run's peerless feats marked the pinnacle for Mullins and her Gold Cup victory was the crowning moment of O'Neill's career. The mare entered the folklore of Irish racing, celebrated for her abundance of qualities, the speed of a brilliant two-mile hurdler, the stamina of an exceptional staying chaser and always the heart of a lion.
ALAN SWEETMAN

POETRY IN MOTION: Dawn Run and Jonjo O'Neill canter to post before the 1986 Gold Cup

MOMENT IN HISTORY: Dawn Run (right) clears the final fence in the 1986 Gold Cup in third place behind Forgive 'N Forget (left) and Wayward Lad before claiming an unforgettable victory

SHE'S MADE IT: Jonjo O'Neill punches the air as Dawn Run returns to a rapturous reception in the hallowed Cheltenham winner's enclosure after the 1986 Gold Cup

# 04

# MIESQUE

Miesque was quite simply a gift from the heavens for an owner-breeder – a precocious talent who flourished into a top-class racehorse before she passed on her immense speed to valuable stallion sons and broodmare daughters.

In conversations with those closest to Francois Boutin, it becomes obvious she was the ultimate expression of her late trainer's talent and understanding for the thoroughbred.

"Miesque was the first yearling out of Pasadoble, who won twice at Listed level and was a very good mare in her own right," recalls Alan Cooper, the longtime racing manager to the Niarchos family, who first went to work for Stavros Niarchos when Miesque was a yearling.

"She was always a little bit masculine and in the yard she was known as 'the concierge' by the staff, because she was always taking note of what was going on around."

Freddy Head rode Miesque in all but one of her races and had a complex relationship with her.

"She was a filly with an enormous amount of speed but she was free running with it, which didn't always make it that comfortable for the jockey," says Head. "I never got full pleasure out of riding her because she was a brute. She pulled hard and getting her covered up wasn't easy. But she was very, very good."

After a winning debut at Deauville in August 1986, Boutin pitched her straight into Group 1 company in the Prix Morny, in which she finished a close third to the Japanese-owned Sakura Reiko, a result that would be reversed in the Prix de la Salamandre and Prix Marcel Boussac that season, as well as in the Poule d'Essai des Pouliches the following May.

A trip to Britain for the 1,000 Guineas was to be

Miesque's first major target at three but, after coming through her prep in the Prix Imprudence, Head was alarmed to find her looking anything but ready for Classic glory at Newmarket.

"I remember before the 1,000 Guineas she still had quite a wintery coat on her and she banged her head in the stable when Francois Boutin was saddling her," says Head.

A furlong and a half out Miesque was still in behind a wall of horses, but as Head angled her left towards the middle of the track the race was as good as over, with good fillies Milligram and Interval left in her wake.

With Sakura Reiko the main opposition once again there was little to fear from attempting to add the French Guineas just over a fortnight later, after which thoughts quickly turned to the Prix de Diane over an extended mile and a quarter.

Henry Cecil sent Indian Skimmer to Chantilly and, determined to try to run the finish out of Miesque, added pacemaker Laluche for good measure.

Despite the generous tempo set by the two raiders, Miesque refused to settle and only her class got her to within four lengths of Indian Skimmer.

Head says: "She was beaten by a very good filly of Sheikh Mohammed's. I tried to cover her up and she was never really going that day. I wondered afterwards if I might have been better letting her stride on."

Miesque had already raced eight times and, now armed with the knowledge that a mile was her best trip, Boutin set his sights on the Prix Jacques le Marois in August. And at Deauville she dominated Nashmeel and 2,000 Guineas winner Don't Forget Me to coast home by three lengths.

But sent off at odds of 1-4, she suffered her only defeat in four meetings with Milligram at Ascot the following month.

"The way she won the Prix Jacques le Marois I think that may have been her best run of all," says Head. "But I was suspended when she ran in the Queen Elizabeth Stakes at Ascot and I remember saying to Steve Cauthen that she would pull hard and that the mile at Ascot might be the limit for her. She never dropped the bit the whole race and it cost her in the final 100 metres."

The meticulous Boutin needed proof before committing her to the Breeders' Cup. "I remember before the Breeders' Cup she did her final workout going left-handed around Les Aigles in thick fog," says Cooper. "I was there with my parents and we only saw the last 100 yards of the gallop. Francois

**Foaled**
March 14, 1984
**Pedigree**
Nureyev – Pasadoble
**Breeder**
Flaxman Holdings Ltd
**Owner**
Stavros Niarchos
**Trainer**
Francois Boutin
**Main jockey**
Freddy Head
**Career record**
12 wins and four places from 16 runs
**Most famous for**
A blistering turn of foot that brought her ten Group 1 victories over three seasons, including back-to-back Breeders' Cup Miles
**Fate at stud**
Proved as talented at stud as on the track – all six of her sons went on to stand at stud

**GETTING ON TOP:**
Miesque and Freddy Head get the better of Milligram and Interval in a thrilling finish to the 1,000 Guineas at Newmarket in 1987

Boutin said 'she's worked well'. That was the green light to go to Hollywood.

"Francois is such a key to the story and sadly cancer took him very early."

In California, Miesque was a different filly to the one at Ascot, surging clear of Show Dancer and Sonic Lady.

"There was a moment when I was a little unhappy in the back straight because I was in among horses who already looked beaten," says Head.

"A tiny gap opened up and it was probably too early, but she shot through it and just took off, winning as she liked."

Miesque amassed a record seven Group 1 wins by the end of her three-year-old campaign, a European record for a filly that would not be matched until Minding in 2016.

But Boutin felt she remained at the top of her game and so a light campaign was mapped out for 1988, with all roads leading back to America for an attempt at a second Breeders' Cup Mile.

Head managed to save Miesque's suspect stamina up in stalking the entire field for her comeback in the Prix d'Ispahan over the intermediate 1m1f trip at Longchamp.

But fans would then have to wait until August and a second win in the Jacques le Marois – this time at the expense of Warning – for another glimpse of Europe's star miler.

And once again her dress rehearsal for the US would go awry, as she flew late in the Prix du Moulin but just failed to reel in Soviet Star, whom she had dismissed contemptuously at Deauville the previous month.

"It was partly my fault because you had to hold her up and there was no pace on," admits Head. "I couldn't get out when I wanted and was a little bit hampered by Cash Asmussen on Soviet Star. After she was beaten in the Moulin de Longchamp, Mr Niarchos thought about retiring her but Francois Boutin insisted she must run again. It threw it down with rain at Louisville, which was something of a worry but she walked it again."

That defeat of Daniel Wildenstein's highly touted Steinlen – who would go on to land the prize the following year – in front of 71,000 fans at Churchill Downs was to be Miesque's swansong.

There may never have been such a stunning combination of prowess on the track and long-term breeding heritage off it in any mare's career.

And there can be little doubt that Francois Boutin was a master at realising her potential in both spheres.
SCOTT BURTON

> "I never got full pleasure out of riding her because she was a brute"

# 05
# TRIPTYCH

It may go against the grain to be elevating to the pantheon of all-time greats a mare who was beaten 27 times in her career, until you remember that old line about lies and statistics.

There are unbeaten horses in the record books who amassed not a fraction of Triptych's impressive body of work and yet retired blemish-free in the mind's eye; with the prolific daughter of Riverman it was all about longevity and degree of difficulty, on both of which counts she qualifies for every top ten ever committed to newsprint or thrashed out across a table by discerning racing folk.

In a career spanning five full seasons in the mid-1980s, the handsome dark bay ran no fewer than 41 times in six countries – a schedule that would leave many modern-day fillies in need of a good lie-down.

As a consequence of what was either an admirable equal opportunities programme or the unfathomable acts of capricious rich men, the 14-time winner had two different owners, three different trainers and 15 different jockeys; yet for all the comings and goings, there was one constant, and that was the degree of talent and application she brought to the racetrack.

Even in a final campaign as a six-year-old, she managed a ninth and last Group 1 victory before the light began to fade; in her prime, she was one of the most durable, successful and uplifting females ever to grace the turf, and had she not come up against two of the most stellar names of the decade, her haul of top prizes might have been even bigger.

It was hardly a surprise that Triptych turned out to be the mare she was, given the blood that coursed through her veins. Bred in Kentucky by

Texas oil billionaire Nelson Bunker Hunt and Edward L Stevenson, she was blessed with the pure class of her sire, the 1972 Poule d'Essai des Poulains winner Riverman, and the true grit of her dam Trillion, who won the Prix Ganay among nine successes from 32 starts; not to mention Trillion's dam Margarethen, who won 16 from 64 in five gruelling American campaigns.

It was this blend of talent and toughness that fuelled the bidding war between Alan Clore and Stavros Niarchos at Keeneland in 1983, which ended with Clore paying $2.15 million for the privilege of sending the desirable yearling to David Smaga in France, in whose care she won on her debut at Deauville, was pipped in a Group 3 and won the Group 1 Prix Marcel Boussac so impressively on her final start that she was rated the best two-year-old of either sex in the country.

Smaga had little time to bask in the glow of success, however. Clore, a notoriously hard man to please, sent Triptych to be trained in Ireland by David O'Brien, for whom she became the first filly to win the Irish 2,000 Guineas.

Only the great Oh So Sharp proved too good for her in the Oaks – albeit by a yawning seven-length margin – but a string of solid efforts in three more Classics yielded no better than a fifth in Law Society's Irish Derby, and two wins from nine starts meant this was far from being the defining portion of her career.

That came when, after an abortive plan to send her to race in the States in 1986, she was rerouted to trainer number three, Patrick Biancone back in France. This time, she was not to be restricted by geographical boundaries, crossing borders for eight of her 11 starts, and although her tally of wins was a mere two – one of them in the humble Group 3 Prix La Coupe – this was the season when she finally imprinted her name on the hearts of race fans in Britain.

Sadly for Triptych, it was also the year of Dancing Brave. Like most, she could never beat the undisputed champion, but in regular defeat she became not only an emerging champion herself but also the touchstone by which the finest middle-distance performances of the era might be judged. Beat her and you could consider yourself special.

Triptych was runner-up to Dancing Brave in the Eclipse, third behind him in the King George and in one of the best Arcs of all time, but she gained her compensation in the Champion Stakes (redirected to the July Course because of refurbishment on the Rowley Mile), displaying a fierce turn of foot

**Foaled**
April 19, 1982
**Pedigree**
Riverman – Trillion
**Breeders**
Nelson Bunker Hunt and
Edward L Stevenson
**Owners**
Alan Clore and
Peter Brant
**Trainers**
David Smaga,
David O'Brien and
Patrick Biancone
**Main jockeys**
Tony Cruz and
Steve Cauthen
**Career record**
14 wins and 19 places
from 41 runs
**Most famous for**
Length of career and
depth of achievement,
even in defeat, capped
by the 1987 Champion
Stakes
**Fate at stud**
Killed in a tragic accident
while expecting her
first foal

**GETTING DOWN TO BUSINESS:** Triptych and Steve Cauthen, one of her 15 jockeys, win the 1987 Matchmaker International (now Juddmonte International) at York

surrounding the three Breeders' Cups, of course, but her win in the Marois remains my favourite."

Preparations for her second Breeders' Cup suffered a blip when Goldikova got run down close home in the Prix de la Forêt and looked to have been dealt a mortal blow when she drew a wide gate at Santa Anita.

Head says: "She was badly drawn and didn't get away too well so Olivier took her back. She was a long way behind before running right past the entire field."

There were two main targets for 2010 – an attempt at a record-breaking third win in the Mile and, before that, a tilt at the Queen Anne Stakes at Royal Ascot in June.

"Ascot is a very stiff mile for a mare like her and she didn't really stay it properly," says Head. "It was a brilliant ride from Olivier, who managed to just conserve her stamina and she won by a neck."

A third Rothschild followed before a combination of Makfi and heavy ground at Deauville did for her in the Marois.

Once more the Forêt on Arc day would be the springboard for America and again Peslier was the man of the moment.

"Olivier rode another brilliant race because she got beaten the year before when leading for most of the race," says Head. "He found himself in front too soon again and he sat absolutely motionless and let another horse come past him.

"He scared the life out of me but he waited and waited before pulling her out again at the first winning post and they went on to win."

History awaited at Churchill Downs, where once again Goldikova found a different way to win, surviving a wide trip into the first turn before unleashing her winning run, trailed home by her delirious groom Thierry Blaise, who danced down the dirt track in pursuit.

"I was very confident going to the Breeders' Cup, as I always was with her," says Head.

Two more Group 1 successes were gained in 2011 – a defeat of Cirrus Des Aigles in the d'Ispahan and a fourth straight win in the Rothschild – as well as defeats at Ascot, Deauville and Longchamp.

That spark of acceleration was just beginning to wane, but the Wertheimers decided to give Goldikova a shot at immortality at the Breeders' Cup. There was no Hollywood ending, but she fought like a lioness to be third.

"She ran a fantastic race," says Head. "Three wins and a third is a record that will last a long time."

SCOTT BURTON

**Foaled**
March 15, 2005
**Pedigree**
Anabaa – Born Gold
**Breeders**
Wertheimer et Frère
**Owners**
Wertheimer et Frère
**Trainer**
Freddy Head
**Jockey**
Olivier Peslier
**Career record**
17 wins and nine places from 27 runs
**Most famous for**
Winning 14 Group 1s and becoming the first horse to win the same Breeders' Cup race three times
**Fate at stud**
Her first foal, a colt by Galileo called Goldikovic, made only two racecourse appearances but his sister Terrakova finished third in the Prix de Diane in June 2017. Has a yearling filly by Intello, Goldika

It would be the only time she finished out of the frame as Peslier wisely looked after her when she failed to pick her legs out of the cloying Longchamp surface.

"It was worse than heavy and she ran badly," says Head. "But you worry with fillies from three to four and it was a far from reassuring effort. We went to Newmarket to see whether she retained her ability and she won the Falmouth Stakes well, so we knew we had her back. She won the Rothschild again – and then in my opinion her win in the Jacques le Marois was the best of her life."

Goldikova was at the peak of her powers and dispatched Aqlaam by six lengths. "She won in a canter and broke the race record," says Head.

That success – she would twice be beaten in the race on soft ground – also ranks as Goldikova's finest hour for Bureau. "It was her most wonderful year and, for me, her greatest performance was in the Marois," he says. "There was a lot of emotion

BATTLE ROYAL: Goldikova (right) beats Paco Boy in the Queen Anne Stakes at Royal Ascot in 2010

STANDING TOGETHER: Goldikova and Olivier Peslier after the filly's second Breeders' Cup Mile success in 2009 at Santa Anita

**TRIPLE TREAT:**
Goldikova and delighted connections after her historic Breeders' Cup Mile success at Churchill Downs in November 2010

# 07
## SUN CHARIOT

No other filly has been both brilliant and erratic to the same extent as Sun Chariot, the wartime Triple Crown winner.

Sir Gordon Richards, who rode her in most of her races, once said: "She was a machine, and what a character. I have a few grey hairs and she gave them to me."

In Phil Bull's words, "She was a curious mixture of extraordinary speed and stamina and tantalising wilfulness."

Although a prima donna, she was also a ray of light in the middle of the war, and her Classic victories in the royal colours boosted popular morale at a critical point in the country's fortunes.

In those days the National Stud was a significant breeder of horses, and the pick of them were leased to King George VI for their racing careers and sent into training with Fred Darling at Beckhampton.

The 1939 crop included Hyperion's daughter Sun Chariot and Big Game, who proved to be outstanding champions in both their seasons on the racecourse.

Darling was a martinet and perfectionist, a trainer who bent humans and horses to his will, and he had no time for those who refused to comply.

He had had to dismiss Sun Chariot's dam, Clarence (named after a type of carriage), who had a temper and never ran. He also gave up on the great filly herself, as she exhibited an unacceptable degree of stubbornness and sheer bloody-mindedness.

She would refuse to go on the gallops, bucking and kicking, swishing her tail like a windmill, perfecting ways of frustrating her riders and upsetting the rest of the string.

Only wartime bureaucracy prevented her dispatch back to the National Stud (based at the time in Ireland) in the spring of 1941, for the necessary export licence was delayed. Before it arrived, Sun Chariot condescended to gallop and showed such startling ability that Darling decided it was worth persevering with her.

After a decisive victory on her debut at Newbury when still unnamed, she ran in the Queen Mary Stakes at Newmarket, where she became unbalanced on the downhill run into the Dip and did not catch Perfect Peace until the final stride.

An effortless win in a minor race at Salisbury was followed by victory over colts in the Middle Park Stakes; she had no trouble in beating subsequent champion Ujiji by three lengths.

She was the champion two-year-old, being rated 1lb ahead of Big Game at the top of the Free Handicap.

Her rider during that campaign was Harry Wragg because Darling's retained jockey, Gordon Richards, had broken a leg. Richards rode her throughout her Classic season.

On her reappearance in 1942 in the Southern Stakes at Salisbury, Richards checked Sun Chariot at one point and she lost interest, refusing to take hold of her bit and dead-heating for third place behind Ujiji.

It was the only defeat of her career and it taught Richards that she needed to be left alone to run her own race without being dictated to by her jockey.

In his autobiography he said: "I was always a little worried by Sun Chariot at the starting-gate. She gave you a nasty feeling going in, always behind her bridle, with her head round on one side, looking at you."

A week after her defeat she returned to Salisbury for the Sarum Stakes. This time she behaved herself in the race and won easily. Sun Chariot had only three more races and they all resulted in Classic victories – in races officially called the New 1,000 Guineas, New Oaks and New St Leger, all of them run on Newmarket's July Course in that wartime season.

In the 1,000 Guineas she caused a little trouble at the start as usual but, in the race, responded as soon as Richards asked for an effort and sprinted four lengths clear of Perfect Peace. This matched Big Game's winning margin in the 2,000 Guineas the previous day.

Soon afterwards the king and queen went to Beckhampton to see Sun Chariot and Big Game work but the filly was on her worst behaviour, taking Richards into a ploughed field, going down on her knees and roaring like a bull.

Despite her temperament, she was a robust

**Foaled**
March 5, 1939
**Pedigree**
Hyperion – Clarence
**Breeder**
National Stud
**Owner**
King George VI
**Trainer**
Fred Darling
**Main jockeys**
Gordon Richards
and Harry Wragg
**Career record**
Eight wins and one third
from nine runs
**Most famous for**
Winning a wartime
Triple Crown in the royal
colours
**Fate at stud**
Produced four high-class
colts, including Sussex
Stakes winner Landau

"She was a curious mixture of extraordinary speed and stamina and tantalising wilfulness"

filly and could take plenty of work – when she wanted to.

An astonishing display in the Oaks typified both her waywardness and her brilliance. The 1-4 favourite dived left when the tapes went up at the start, losing many lengths and almost causing Richards to give up hope, and she also ran wide turning into the long straight.

When she eventually caught her rivals she went straight past them, but had to be ridden out with hands and heels to hold off Afterthought by a length. The king himself, in RAF uniform, led her in.

Her wilfulness meant that she had had a harder race than necessary, and it may have cost her the Derby the following day.

With an effortless Oaks victory Darling might have allowed her to contest the Derby, but in the end Big Game was his only runner – and he failed to stay, finishing sixth.

Sun Chariot gradually became more amenable and gave no trouble either in her preparation for the St Leger or in the race itself. She outclassed the first two in the Derby, Watling Street and Hyperides, by three lengths and five to become the first fillies' Triple Crown winner since Pretty Polly 38 years before.

Sun Chariot and Big Game had won four of the five Classics between them, which made the king champion owner and Darling champion trainer, as well as helping Richards to the 15th of his 26 jockeys' titles.

Seven of Sun Chariot's ten foals to race turned out to be winners and four of them were high-class colts – unbeaten Blue Train, Gigantic (Imperial Stakes), Landau (Sussex Stakes) and St Leger third Pindari. She also bred Persian Wheel, fourth in the 1,000 Guineas. She died in 1963, aged 24.

JOHN RANDALL

**ROYAL RESULT**
King George VI, in RAF uniform, leads in Sun Chariot after her Oaks win at Newmarket in 1942

# 08

# OUIJA BOARD

Ouija Board plundered such an embarrassment of riches over four seasons that connections find it difficult to settle on their favourite memory.

Trainer Ed Dunlop inclines towards the 2006 Prince of Wales's Stakes before reminding himself that she won the Breeders' Cup Filly & Mare Turf twice – "and she was unlucky not to win a third," he reflects. "Mind you, she was my first British Classic winner when she won the Oaks."

Owner-breeder Lord Derby considers the question before highlighting her pulsating duel with another globetrotter, Alexander Goldrun, in the 2006 Nassau Stakes. "That was one of the truly great finishes," he recalls. "There was also the first of her Breeders' Cup

wins at Lone Star Park [in Texas], which was a fantastic experience." In the end, however, the 19th earl gravitates closer to home. "To win the Classic named after the family place at Epsom was an amazing experience," he says.

The Oaks was an estate near Epsom that was leased by Lord Derby's ancestor, the 12th earl, who devised the race in 1778 and won its first running the following year with Bridget. He was also instrumental in the Derby's inauguration in 1780, and Ouija Board's son, Australia, won that race ten years after she had won the Oaks.

It was in the Oaks that Ouija Board first announced her uncommon prowess. It was the first Group race she contested, having won Newmarket's Pretty Polly Stakes on her sophomore debut.

"As a two-year-old she was decent, no more than that," Dunlop reflects. "We knew she'd have to stay to be better than that at three, but it wasn't clear from her pedigree whether she would."

However, Dunlop was emboldened by a gallop Ouija Board completed before her three-year-old campaign. "Kieren Fallon came in to ride her on the Cambridge Road Polytrack and he said he'd ridden the Oaks favourite, who was trained by Sir Michael Stoute, earlier that morning and Ouija Board was the better filly."

Fallon's view was endorsed at Epsom and again at the Curragh, where Ouija Board followed up, albeit less spectacularly, in the Irish Oaks. All roads then led to the Prix de l'Arc de Triomphe

> "She was explosive at the end of her races and that made for some tremendously exciting finishes"

and, with Fallon unavailable, Johnny Murtagh was legged up for the first time.

"Eight different jockeys rode Ouija Board," Lord Derby says, "and many of them said she wasn't an easy ride. She would take them further back in a race than they expected."

Ouija Board was certainly far back as the Arc field swung for home. She had 13 horses to pass down the straight and managed to overhaul most of them before finishing third, a length and a half behind Bago. "On balance, I feel she would probably have won if she hadn't got so far back," Dunlop says, "but she's by no means the first horse that has happened to at Longchamp."

Ouija Board lost nothing in defeat, and a light three-year-old campaign made a tilt at the Breeders' Cup a tempting proposition even though she had to be supplemented expensively into the Filly & Mare Turf.

What a day it was. Never in the slightest danger of defeat, Ouija Board moved up to challenge early in the home straight under Fallon and quickly imposed her authority to win by a length and a half. If the Oaks had telegraphed her class, the Breeders' Cup amplified that she had the mental and physical attributes to advance still further.

Those attributes were tested to the hilt after Ouija Board's seasonal debut at four. She lost a front shoe and tailed herself off in the Prince of Wales's Stakes, which was run at York in 2005 while Ascot was being rebuilt. Loose ground on top exacerbated her plight, and she returned home with a hairline fracture that would detain her for more than three months.

When she returned, under Frankie Dettori for the first time, Ouija Board made light of her absence to land the Princess Royal Stakes at Newmarket in September. She was back in business.

That Newmarket victory marked the last time British racegoers would see Ouija Board for nine months. She travelled from the US to Japan and on to Dubai via Hong Kong, after which she returned to Hong Kong once more.

In terms of placings, her worst effort came when she finished fifth in the Japan Cup, for which she earned £127,000. Her best saw her waltz away with the Hong Kong Vase by two and three-quarter lengths on her final start at four. That banked her a handsome £536,000.

There were some hard-luck stories, although Ouija Board's style of racing lent itself to running into trouble. "She had that tremendous burst of speed," recalls Lord Derby. "She was explosive at

**Foaled**
March 6, 2001
**Pedigree**
Cape Cross – Selection Board
**Breeder**
Stanley Estate & Stud Co
**Owner**
Lord Derby
**Trainer**
Ed Dunlop
**Main jockeys**
Kieren Fallon and Frankie Dettori
**Career record**
Ten wins and eight places from 22 runs
**Most famous for**
Winning seven Group/Grade 1 races in four countries; her son Australia became the only horse by a Derby winner out of a non-promoted winner of the Oaks to win the Derby
**Fate at stud**
Dam of seven foals and five runners to date; all winners, including Australia (won Derby, Irish Derby, International Stakes) and Our Voodoo Prince (Australian G3 winner)

the end of her races and that made for some tremendously exciting finishes. There were times when she might have been hard done by but we also had some lucky breaks."

When Ouija Board resurfaced in Britain for the 2006 Coronation Cup, she never really threatened to overhaul Shirocco. The thought occurred that her extensive travels might have taken a toll, yet her next start proved a revelation.

She was opposed by a slew of hard-hitting colts in the Prince of Wales's Stakes but overcame a steady gallop to glide past Electrocutionist and Manduro down the Ascot straight under Olivier Peslier.

"I remember screaming my head off as she started making ground around the bend," Lord Derby says. "It was another great memory, especially after what had happened 12 months earlier at York."

Ouija Board ran in five more races after Royal Ascot, winning the aforementioned Nassau Stakes and a second Filly & Mare Turf. Her career-closing start was scheduled for the Hong Kong Vase she'd won the previous year. Alas, however, Ouija Board aggravated a splint when posting a stunning time in her final gallop at Sha Tin, and was retired with total earnings in excess of £3.5 million.

Yet that reverse spawned a new, as-yet-unfinished chapter. Ouija Board made a seamless transition from outstanding racemare to outstanding broodmare, thanks principally to Australia's dual Derby heroics in 2014.

"I can't tell you how many tears flowed at Epsom that day," Lord Derby says. "My uncle, John, tried all his life to breed a Derby winner. It was the first Derby win for the family at Epsom since Hyperion in 1933, although Watling Street won the wartime substitute at Newmarket in 1942."

And the story has far from run its course. In partnership with Bill Gredley, Lord Derby has in training Big Blue, an unraced three-year-old by Dubawi out of Ouija Board. There's a yearling filly by Dubawi to come, and Ouija Board, who had no foal in 2016, is awaiting a return date with the same sire.

"At the time Ouija Board was my only horse in training," Lord Derby reflects. "The whole episode has been a mind-boggling experience, just amazing all the way, and what I find hard to believe is that it is now ten years since she retired from the racetrack. The memories are so fresh, so vivid."

It will be many years hence before Ouija Board's dazzling exploits recede into the mists of time.
JULIAN MUSCAT

JOB DONE: Ouija Board wins the Breeders' Cup Filly & Mare Turf for the first time at Lone Star Park in Texas in October 2004

HEAD TO HEAD: Ouija Board and Frankie Dettori (far side) hold on from Alexander Goldrun and Kevin Manning in a memorable finish to the Nassau Stakes at Glorious Goodwood in August 2006

MISSION ACCOMPLISHED: Ouija Board and Frankie Dettori are led down the track after her victory in the Filly & Mare Turf at Churchill Downs in 2006

# 09
## TREVE

Not all champions are flawless in design. Some come with imperfections, mental and physical, and only in the right hands do they reach their true potential.

In the last 39 years, Treve is the only horse – male or female – to win back-to-back Arcs, yet the way she went about her business was far from conventional.

Considering she was a daughter of quirky Derby winner Motivator, himself a son of the mercurial but supreme Montjeu, perhaps it is unsurprising Treve was not an image of perfection.

Often awash with sweat on the big days, she was a free traveller who pulled like a mine train with no breaks, her head hanging awkwardly high in the process. Yet beyond those quirks lay an engine fit for the Rolls-Royce production line. All it needed was to be handled with care.

Treve was an undoubted triumph for the Head family. Bred by Alec Head at the family's Haras du Quesnay in Deauville and trained by his daughter Criquette Head-Maarek, Treve had just the one run at two, winning over a mile at Longchamp before retiring for the winter.

Her Classic season started with a low-key success at Saint-Cloud, but hopes of running in the Group 1 Prix de Diane were threatened when she returned a sick horse. Time was against her but with the Diane fast approaching, Treve started to come right and Head-Maarek made the bold decision to run.

"Papa thought it was too much," she says. "There was a stakes race two weeks before, but it was too close so I decided to go straight to the Diane."

The lack of match practice proved inconsequential as Treve burst through to lead well over a fur-long out to register an impressive victory on just her third career start, her first beyond a mile and first at Group level.

The Prix de l'Opera would surely have been Treve's for the taking after such an impressive performance, but with Al Shaqab Racing now on board bolder plans were hatched with Europe's greatest open-age middle-distance race, the Prix de l'Arc de Triomphe, emerging as the preferred end-of-season target.

The decision to stump up the €100,000 supplementary fee was an easy one after she easily landed the Vermeille under Al Shaqab's retained rider Frankie Dettori for the first time.

Preparing for his 26th consecutive appearance in the Arc, Dettori was cruelly ruled out after a tumble on his way to post for a 0-75 handicap at Nottingham four days before left him with a broken bone in his foot.

Regular rider Thierry Jarnet was reunited with Treve and, in what was widely billed as a strong Arc, she was sent off 9-2 second favourite behind the previous year's unlucky runner-up Orfevre.

What those present on that crisp autumn afternoon at Longchamp witnessed was not just one of the greatest performances in the race's history but one of the best middle-distance performances of the modern day.

Considering she sweated up, was trapped wide from stall 15 and failed to settle, it is still hard to fathom how she passed the post five lengths clear of runner-up Orfevre, one of the best horses to come out of Japan.

"I thought she had six gears, but she put seven gears on," says Head-Maarek. "She was never covered up and had to come on the outside but when a horse is that good it makes no difference."

If that performance still takes some believing, the fact she turned up on Arc day the following year having suffered three straight defeats is even more dumbfounding.

Dettori, having ridden Treve just days before her reappearance in the Prix Ganay, felt she was "unbeatable" according to her trainer, such was her wellbeing at the start of her third season. But in granite-tough veteran Cirrus Des Aigles she met a formidable opponent with race-fitness on his side,

### "It is difficult to find a word to describe what she has done and what she means to everyone"

**Foaled**
April 7, 2010
**Pedigree**
Motivator – Trevise
**Breeder**
Haras du Quesnay
**Owner**
Al Shaqab Racing
**Trainer**
Criquette Head-Maarek
**Jockeys**
Thierry Jarnet and Frankie Dettori
**Career record**
Nine wins and two places from 13 runs
**Most famous for**
Winning back-to-back Prix de l'Arc de Triomphes among six Group 1 wins
**Fate at stud**
Whisked off to Sheikh Joaan Al Thani's Haras de Bouquetot following her retirement, Treve was scanned in foal for the first time in April 2016 and her eagerly awaited colt foal by star stallion Dubawi was born in February 2017

**EMOTIONAL SCENE:**
Thierry Jarnet salutes the crowd as he returns on Treve to the winner's enclosure at Longchamp after their first success in the Prix de l'Arc de Triomphe in 2013

and with gritted teeth he inflicted a first defeat on Treve in a humdinger.

Back and foot problems were blamed for two further defeats at Royal Ascot and in the Prix Vermielle, by which time Dettori had been relegated to the subs' bench for Jarnet.

"A lot of people said she was gone, she was no good, but I asked Sheikh Joaan just to have faith in me," recalls Head-Maarek.

Rated an 11-1 shot this time in a typically strong Arc line-up, Treve was her usual edgy self in the preliminaries. Awash with sweat by the time she reached the start, she was also back to her old self in the race.

As had been the case 12 months earlier, she took a strong grip but on this occasion enjoyed a much kinder trip around the inside, and when a gap appeared with less than two furlongs to run Jarnet unleashed her trademark turn of foot, sending her clear and into the record books as only the seventh dual winner of the Arc and the first to complete the double since Alleged in 1977 and 1978.

Head-Maarek, winning her third Arc, described the victory as the best of her career and, in a blaze of glory, Treve was retired. Or so we thought.

A conversation with Alec Head when Sheikh Joaan visited his retired champion the day after the Arc appears to have been the catalyst for a dramatic U-turn and six days later came the announcement that retirement was on hold and a quest for racing immortality and an unprecedented third win in the Arc was on.

Free from any ailments, her build-up was smooth this time, Treve winning without fuss on three runs before her date with destiny.

This time it was Jarnet who felt Treve was "unbeatable", which according to her trainer was the reason the rider was happy to take up a position out wide, similar to their first success.

On this occasion, however, the history-maker was Golden Horn, with Treve running below her very best. She still finished a close fourth, making strong headway up the home straight, but was unable to claw back the Derby winner.

In truth, being beaten just over two lengths by an exceptional champion, with Flintshire and New Bay also in front, meant she lost little in defeat on her final start, with Treve retiring as the winner of nine of her 13 races with more than £6 million in prize-money in the bank.

"For me she was exceptional," says her trainer. "It is difficult to find a word to describe what she has done and what she means to everyone. Elle est fantastique."
**LEWIS PORTEOUS**

WORM'S EYE VIEW: Thierry Jarnet and Treve record a comfortable six-length victory in the Prix Vermeille at Longchamp in September 2015

CROWNING GLORY: Treve saves her best until last as she rediscovers her magic to record back-to-back Arcs at Longchamp in October 2014

HEAD HELD HIGH: all eyes are on Treve after her second success in the Arc in October 2014

# 10
# BLACK CAVIAR

Australia had never seen anything like Black Caviar, and frankly neither had the rest of us. The 'Wonder from Down Under' utterly transcended the sport in her home country as she compiled a world-famous unbeaten sequence stretching to 25 races.

She went into retirement in April 2013 as a household name on all four corners of the racing globe, one of the greatest sprinters of all time, and one of the most popular, a towering reputation not a whit diminished by her close shave at Royal Ascot in 2012 when jockey Luke Nolen suffered his notorious 'brain fade'.

Not for nothing is she the highest-rated filly or mare in the history of Racing Post Ratings and a four-time world champion sprinter.

Every inch an equine superstar, Black Caviar was a sporting and cultural phenomenon in Australia, where she established the longest winning streak in the nation's history. She won 15 Group 1s, eclipsing the Australian record of triple Cox Plate hero Kingston Town; when she won eight in a row, she beat the record established by Bernborough in 1946.

In the process, she became pure box-office, as dazzling a racehorse as you could hope to see. Despite facing the best sprinters in a nation justifiably revered for its prowess in that division, Black Caviar generally won without breaking sweat at odds as short as 1-33 on the local tote. In fact, she was made favourite for every single one of her 25 races, being sent off odds-on for the last 24.

Black Caviar was a world champion, but more than that she was the people's champion, taken to the hearts of an adoring Aussie public who speak of her exploits in the same breath as the legendary depression-era hero Phar Lap.

Described as a "once-in-a-generation" racehorse by Racing Victoria handicapper Greg Carpenter, Black Caviar single-handedly propelled horseracing back into the mainstream Aussie psyche.

Timepieces could be set by Black Caviar: two furlongs out, when the heat was at its most intense, that's where she turned on the afterburners to destroy her rivals, damage done in a couple of those powerful strides.

Black Caviar's syndicate owners blew their budget to buy the daughter of Group 1-winning sprinter Bel Esprit: they had planned to spend no more than A$125,000 (£78,000) but she cost A$210,000 (£132,000) at the Inglis Melbourne Premier Yearling Sale in 2008.

Known as 'Nelly' at Moody's Melbourne stable, Black Caviar was restricted to just five starts in her first two seasons. While in retrospect they look pretty auspicious – she won a Listed race by six lengths on her final juvenile start, and landed a couple of Group 2s at three – it was during her four- and five-year-old campaigns that the Black Caviar legend was to be written as she earned her place in racing folklore with a series of breathtaking victories in Australia.

Eight wins as a four-year-old in 2010–11 were followed by eight more in 2011–12 as she embarked on what amounted to a two-year national tour of four different states before she came to Royal Ascot.

Three times she was to win the Lightning Stakes, the nation's most prestigious sprint at Flemington, where she also produced an electrifying weight-carrying performance in the Newmarket Handicap of March 2011 to record a RPR of 133 after giving Crystal Lily the small matter of 18lb – and a three-length beating, in race-record time. That rating, hit for a second time the same year in the TJ Smith Stakes at Randwick, was to be the highest of her career; it remains the best RPR for a sprinter since Dayjur's 136 in 1990.

In second place in the Sydney contest was Hay List, a top-class sprinter whose destiny it was to play the Washington General to Black Caviar's Harlem Globetrotter. Time after time dismissed with contempt, he finished second to her four times, and was left eating her dust six times altogether.

**Foaled**
August 18, 2006
**Pedigree**
Bel Esprit – Helsinge
**Breeder**
Rick Jamieson
**Owners**
GJ Wilkie, KJ Wilkie, Werrett Bloodstock Pty Ltd, CH Madden, J Madden, PA Hawkes, DM Taylor and J Taylor
**Trainer**
Peter Moody
**Main jockey**
Luke Nolen
**Career record**
25 wins from 25 runs
**Most famous for**
Four-time world champion sprinter never beaten in 25-race career, including a dramatic visit to Royal Ascot in 2012
**Fate at stud**
Oscietra, her first foal by Exceed And Excel, finished third on her debut for the Hayes/Dabernig stable at Flemington on New Year's Day 2017; she also has progeny by Sebring and Snitzel

> "Every inch an equine superstar, [she] was a sporting and cultural phenomenon"

And this was a three-time Group 1-winning sprinter in his own right.

Her arrival in Britain for Royal Ascot for the Diamond Jubilee Stakes was greeted with the sort of feverish excitement more usually associated with a Hollywood star attending a Leicester Square premiere.

Royal Ascot stood as a place transformed thanks to the influx of thousands of her ex-pat countrymen making the pilgrimage; a distinctly Aussie sense of pageantry prevailed as the traditional red, white and blue hues were changed overnight to salmon-pink and black.

In the event, like everything else she was over-shadowed by Frankel's Queen Anne romp but, given the circumstances, she let nobody down in a victory unlike any other Black Caviar victory, owing rather more to guts and determination than blistering talent as Nolen threw the reins at her in the dying strides after dropping his hands.

After a desperate dive for the line on unsuitably rain-softened turf, she held on by a head from French-trained Moonlight Cloud.

Yet while Black Caviar may not have scorched the Berkshire turf she seared an indelible mark on racing's collective memory. She came, she saw and she conquered. And even if she conquered her Ascot opponents by mere inches, she conquered our affections by many a mile on a day never likely to be forgotten by anybody there. Or by those among the thousands watching on a big screen at midnight in Melbourne's Federation Square.

However, Australia's sweetheart had been pulled to pieces at Ascot, aching muscles torn apart. Post-race X-rays revealed she had sustained an eight-centimetre muscle tear somewhere in the race and any notion of a great career being extended into a fifth season appeared fanciful indeed when the mighty mare returned home a shadow of her former self.

Return she did, though, after an eight-month absence for an abbreviated six-year-old campaign taking in three Group 1 races, two in Melbourne and one in Sydney. After an exhibition gallop at Caulfield, Black Caviar duly reappeared before a huge crowd at Flemington to contest the Lightning Stakes, which had been renamed in her honour.

In a display of breathtaking arrogance befitting a 1-10 favourite, she proceeded to break the track record with a time of 55.47 sec for 1,000 metres (just short of five furlongs), bettering a mark that had stood for 25 years. By any standards, this was a superlative comeback, better than anybody dared imagine – and her connections started to discuss the possibility of a return visit to Britain in the summer. Until, that is, they caught everyone unawares by finally pulling the plug after another victory in the TJ Smith Stakes, where she extended her celebrated unbeaten record to 25.

"It was a hard decision but we just thought the time was right," said Moody. "We've done our job, she's more than done hers, she's been a great advocate for the sport. She brought interest to our sport that hasn't been there for decades. Black Caviars don't come along every day."

Indeed they do not.

NICHOLAS GODFREY

**CENTRE OF ATTENTION:** Black Caviar and Luke Nolen return to a packed winner's enclosure after her extraordinary success in the Diamond Jubilee Stakes at Royal Ascot in the summer of 2012

STRUNG OUT: Black Caviar wins her 23rd consecutive race when romping home in the Lightning Stakes, named in her honour, at Flemington in February 2013. She went on to make it 25 out of 25 before retiring two months later

THAT WAS CLOSE: a relieved Luke Nolen with Black Caviar's connections after the Diamond Jubilee Stakes

ON THE LINE: in a desperately close finish, Black Caviar holds on to win by a head from Moonlight Cloud (far right, white cap) at Royal Ascot in 2012

# 11
# PETITE ETOILE

Petite Etoile was wilful and highly strung, a prima donna who contrived to be at the centre of attention even in defeat.

The 1,000 Guineas and Oaks heroine of 1959 possessed a brilliant turn of foot that Lester Piggott repeatedly utilised so that she came late and won on a tight rein by a narrow margin, which added to the drama of her appearances.

For all her quirks, the grey was game and wonderfully consistent, never finishing out of the first two in her 19 races, and regularly beat colts, including in the Sussex and Champion Stakes and two Coronation Cups. She also broke the British prize-money record for a filly or mare.

She was the darling of racecourse crowds for most of her four seasons, and was never less than a celebrity.

Petite Etoile, whose fourth dam was the legendary Mumtaz Mahal, was bred by Aga Khan III and his son Prince Aly Khan, and ran in the latter's name for most of her career.

Put into training with Noel Murless in Newmarket, she was not tested against the best as a two-year-old, being regarded as a sprinter rather than a Classic prospect. She was rated 15lb below the champion in the official ratings.

Yet in 1959 she landed the Free Handicap and then triumphed by a length in the 1,000 Guineas under Doug Smith after Piggott had chosen to ride another Murless filly.

Jockey and horse were reunited in the Oaks, in which the firm ground helped her to overcome doubts about her stamina; she hacked up by three lengths from Cantelo, who went on to win the St Leger. It was a vintage crop of Classic fillies but Petite Etoile was supreme.

She completed an unbeaten campaign with effortless narrow-margin victories in the Sussex Stakes, Yorkshire Oaks and Champion Stakes, although at Newmarket Piggott nearly contrived to get himself boxed in in a three-horse race.

In his autobiography, Piggott described her as "undoubtedly the greatest of her sex that I rode" and said she was "a bit of a monkey, ready to lark about if her rider was not wary: we always had to be very careful with her at home and let her have her own way now and again".

Murless once remarked: "She was a peculiar animal. She was a grey and she loved to have a grey in front of her in the string and, more particularly, a grey behind her when she went out to exercise. In my experience this was unique but then Petite Etoile was unique in every way."

Aly Khan was killed in a car crash in Paris in May 1960, so she subsequently ran in the name of first his executors, then his son, the present Aga Khan.

In the Coronation Cup Petite Etoile outclassed Parthia, the previous year's Derby winner, but then, in the most controversial of her five defeats, she came second when 2-5 favourite for the King George VI and Queen Elizabeth Stakes.

Last of all turning for home, she found her path on the inside blocked early in the short straight and was bumped, and when pulled to the outside she failed by half a length to peg back mudlark Aggressor.

Piggott was heavily criticised for giving her too much to do and meeting trouble in running, but the soft ground blunted her acceleration and put the emphasis on stamina over a trip that was beyond her best.

Coughing ended Petite Etoile's 1960 campaign but she was kept in training as a five-year-old in order to stimulate her young owner's interest in the sport. She started by winning the Coronation (now Brigadier Gerard) Stakes at Sandown, the Coronation Cup again and the Rous Memorial Stakes at Royal Ascot.

She had often given the impression of having a large amount in hand, which enhanced her aura of invincibility. Yet it gradually became apparent that

> "She had often given the impression of having a large amount in hand, which enhanced her aura of invincibility"

ULTRA-CONSISTENT:
Petite Etoile (right) never finished worse than second and won 14 of her 19 races

she was a free runner who found little off the bridle, was increasingly vulnerable with age and found 1m4f beyond her comfort zone.

These awkward facts had contributed to her King George defeat, and became even clearer in the Aly Khan International Memorial Gold Cup at Kempton (with a prize subscribed by friends of her late owner-breeder), in which Sir Winston Churchill's High Hat led all the way and ran her into the ground.

Petite Etoile then won the Scarbrough Stakes at Doncaster but ended her career with defeat by Le Levanstell in the Queen Elizabeth II Stakes. The spark had gone.

At stud she had only one winner from her three surviving foals, but the Aga Khan persevered with her family and she eventually became the fifth dam of his unbeaten Arc winner Zarkava. She died in 1978, aged 22.

JOHN RANDALL

**Foaled**
1956
**Pedigree**
Petition – Star Of Iran
**Breeders**
Prince Aly Khan and
Aga Khan III
**Owners**
Prince Aly Khan and
Aga Khan IV
**Trainer**
Noel Murless
**Main jockeys**
Lester Piggott
and Doug Smith
**Career record**
14 wins and five seconds
from 19 runs
**Most famous for**
A dual Classic winner
with a brilliant turn of
foot, and a wilful, highly
strung nature
**Fate at stud**
Initially disappointing
but became fifth dam
of Zarkava

# 12

# ZARKAVA

The images remain imperishable from that grey Arc afternoon when Zarkava lit up Longchamp for the final time: of the chestnut's daisy-cutter low stride; of an overcome Christophe Soumillon flinging his helmet into the crowd, then later gathering infant daughter Charley into his arms to ensure she would be part of the photographic legacy of the day.

Trainer Alain de Royer-Dupre thought he had a nice filly when sending Zarkava to Longchamp for her debut at the beginning of September 2007 but, along with her owner-breeder the Aga Khan, he was quickly forced to revise his opinion upwards as the decision was made to supplement her for the Prix Marcel Boussac on Arc day in 2007.

"We had four weeks to play with, which allowed us to give her two tests," says Royer-Dupre. "Firstly we took her back racing at Longchamp to make sure she remained calm. Then 13 days before the Group 1 she did a racecourse gallop at Chantilly with some older horses and she worked magnificently.

"In the Marcel Boussac she jumped a shadow near the line, which showed she was doing it almost too easily. She was still looking around a lot and was by no means getting tired."

Royer-Dupre was to have plenty of sleepless nights with a filly he describes as manic who had to have a padded entrance laid for her box to prevent her from charging into her stable precipitously.

Work-rider Eric Alloix was entrusted with the delicate balancing act of getting her tuned up on Les Aigles without overdoing it, and Royer-Dupre recalls: "He never went too fast with her in the mornings. A horse like her with so much energy – almost a supernatural ability – you really need to protect them in training."

Zarkava showed she could cope with heavy ground in the Prix de la Grotte on her first run at three, and then handed out a beating to the soon-to-be-legendary Goldikova in the Poule d'Essai des Pouliches, a result she would repeat in the Prix de Diane.

"It was a very good generation among the fillies, and for me one of her most impressive performances was in the Poule d'Essai des Pouliches," says Royer-Dupre.

"She was a long way back from Goldikova turning into the straight and, even though it was over that filly's best trip, Zarkava reeled her in very easily. I never had any doubts about her going up in trip for the Prix de Diane but I always think of it as her least spectacular performance.

"She won well but it was on very quick ground and the track was not in perfect condition. She didn't really have the best action that day and she only won because she was a true champion."

After fly-jumping the shadow as a juvenile Zarkava had shown little signs of her difficult nature away from the confines of Aiglemont, but in the Prix Vermeille she almost fell asleep in the stalls before passing the entire field with an irresistible burst of acceleration late on.

"It was a delicate situation in the weeks running up to the race and I would say it was the only time we had trouble doing what we needed to with her before she ran," says her trainer.

"She was too fresh and almost running away with Christophe on the way to post. That is why he tried to restrain her at the start, leading to her standing still.

"But the way she finished in the straight was amazing and that was when you realised you were watching a filly who was completely out of the ordinary.

"Coming down off the stands I could tell from the people around me that everyone felt they had seen something very special."

From the stands on Arc day Zarkava's perfect seven looked anything but assured as she was once again awkwardly away and then stuck in any amount of trouble until well inside the

**"It is so rare to have a horse that good who can complete their career over every trip without being beaten"**

**Foaled**
March 31, 2005
**Pedigree**
Zamindar – Zarkasha
**Breeder**
The Aga Khan
**Owner**
The Aga Khan
**Trainer**
Alain de Royer-Dupre
**Jockey**
Christophe Soumillon
**Career record**
Seven wins from
seven runs
**Famous for**
An extraordinary
unbeaten career which
took in the French fillies'
Triple Crown before
reaching its zenith in
the Arc
**Fate at stud**
After her first four foals
failed to reach the
racecourse, her Dubawi
colt Zarak restored family
honour in 2016 when
finishing second to the
outstanding Almanzor in
the Prix du Jockey Club.
Zarak won the Grand
Prix de Saint-Cloud in
July 2017 while Zarkava's
most recent arrivals are
a Frankel filly in 2015 and
a colt by Invincible Spirit
in 2016

two-furlong marker, but Royer-Dupre never had any doubts.

"After the Vermeille she came out of the race in magnificent condition and we were heading to the Arc safe in the knowledge she was in top form," he says. "The ground got pretty soft but she adapted to everything and she won very easily with a lot up her sleeve. When you have that much energy and that much class, you can take any gap you want to."

Moments after she crossed the line the Aga

**WINNING FEELING:**
a joyous Christophe Soumillon prepares to throw his helmet into the crowd after Zarkava's wonder show in the 2008 Prix de l'Arc de Triomphe at Longchamp

Khan declared that Zarkava represented "the apogee of 80 or 90 years of my family's efforts in breeding", and there never seemed much doubt that she would now head to the paddocks.

Royer-Dupre says: "Those were the most magnificent moments and it is so rare to have a horse that good who can complete their career over every trip without being beaten."
SCOTT BURTON

OUT IN FRONT:
Zarkava and Christophe
Soumillon complete
a stunning victory in
the 2008 Arc

# 13
## RUFFIAN

Often labelled North America's greatest female racehorse, Ruffian became the folk heroine of US racing in the mid-1970s. After a career brutally cut short after just 14 months, her popular appeal rivalled that of even the legendary Secretariat, to whom she can legitimately be seen as a female equivalent, her lustre undimmed even as her achievements recede down the gunsight of history.

An intimidating jet-black specimen, Ruffian was big, beautiful and boy was she fast. She was never headed at a marker pole in any of her races and her US past-performance charts reading as a series of '1's.

She won her first ten races by a cumulative total of 83 lengths but her 11th was to end in tragic circumstances as she suffered a fatal breakdown mid-race in a much-publicised match race at Belmont Park against the 1975 Kentucky Derby winner Foolish Pleasure. It was the only race she ever lost, and she could not be saved after surgery.

Ruffian's old-school trainer was Frank Whiteley, who died aged 93 in April 2008. Twenty-five years after her death, Whiteley recalled seeing the filly for the first time in a field at Claiborne, saying: "She was only a yearling, but she had that quality you only see once in a lifetime. She was a grand-looking filly, you couldn't help but like her – but you couldn't tell if she could run or not!"

Ruffian could run all right. Bigger than most colts with hugely powerful hindquarters yet graceful with it, she went undefeated and virtually unchallenged in her first ten starts with a string of all-the-way victories for owner-breeders Stuart and Barbara Janney, part of the Phipps dynasty.

She was utterly merciless in five races as a two-year-old, even equalling the track record at Belmont

> "Ruffian could run all right. Bigger than most colts with hugely powerful hindquarters yet graceful with it"

**Foaled**
April 17, 1972
**Pedigree**
Reviewer – Shenanigans
**Breeders**
Stuart and
Barbara Janney
**Owners**
Stuart and
Barbara Janney
**Trainer**
Frank Whiteley
**Main jockey**
Jacinto Vasquez
**Career record**
Ten wins from 11 runs
**Most famous for**
Renowned as the greatest
filly in North American
history, a female version
of Secretariat who won
her first ten starts by a
cumulative 83 lengths;
the only race she lost was
the one in which she lost
her life in July 1975

**ONE OF THE BEST:**
Ruffian is often labelled
North America's greatest
female racehorse after
ten wins from 11 starts

Aqueduct in April before making mincemeat of the opposition in what was then known as the New York Filly Triple Crown, a series of prestigious Grade 1 events for three-year-old fillies comprising the Acorn Stakes, Mother Goose Stakes and Coaching Club American Oaks.

Next came the fateful 'Great Match' against Foolish Pleasure over a mile and a quarter at Belmont in July 1975. Coming in the wake of the much-hyped 'Battle of the Sexes' tennis encounter between Billie-Jean King and Bobby Riggs, the $350,000 head-to-head was surrounded by a veritable media circus; fans picked sides and wore button badges as more than 50,000 headed out to Belmont as an estimated 20 million watched on TV.

Riding a tidal wave of public affection, Ruffian was sent off 2-5 favourite. Although she broke slightly awkwardly, she soon had her nose in front of Foolish Pleasure as the pair sprinted from the gate, blazing through the first quarter-mile.

Ruffian had edged a half-length ahead on the inner when tragedy struck amid a sickening mess of shattered sesamoids and ruptured tendons and ligaments.

Even though her off-fore was smashed to pieces, in perhaps the most ghastly part of a horrific incident, jockey Jacinto Vasquez could not pull her up "until she had driven the tip of her splintered cannon bone into the sandy Belmont ground," according to the *Daily Racing Form*'s Jay Hovdey.

Although Ruffian was to survive an emergency operation, she had to be put down after she became violent in the post-operative period and undid all the surgeons' work. She was buried near the flagpole on the Belmont infield.

Two days after her death, Whiteley glanced at her old box and said: "That stall will never be occupied as long as I have this barn. There'll never be another horse worthy of entering it."

She went straight into the Hall of Fame in 1976 and she was the highest-ranked female on the Blood-Horse's list of the Top 100 Racehorses of the 20th Century at number 35.

She was in 53rd place in the *Sports Illustrated* list of the Top 100 female athletes of the century, the only non-human to be featured, and her story was told in a 2007 movie.

But perhaps the final word on such a great filly should come from Lucien Laurin, the trainer of Secretariat.

"As God is my judge, she might be better than Secretariat," he said.
NICHOLAS GODFREY

on her debut in May 1974. She went on to win four Graded stakes that year finishing up with an astonishing near 13-length victory in track-record time in the Grade 1 Spinaway at Saratoga before a hairline fracture of her off-hind ankle ended her season in August.

Just short of eight months later, Ruffian was back as good as ever, winning a couple of races at

# 14

## SCEPTRE

Sceptre is one of those rare champions whose exploits echo down the years, a legendary filly whose name is a byword for class and toughness.

This iron lady won all the Classics except the Derby in 1902, and her record would have been even better had she been trained and ridden competently throughout her career.

If her breeder, the Duke of Westminster, had not died when she was a foal she would have gone into training with John Porter and, according to George Lambton, "she would probably never have been beaten." Her moderate statistics (13 wins, 12 defeats) resulted from the failings of humans, not herself.

Sceptre had an unbeatable pedigree, being by Persimmon out of a sister to Ormonde, and she fetched a world-record price for a yearling at auction when Bob Sievier paid 10,000 guineas for her in 1900.

More than almost any other great champion she had her career influenced by the identity of her owner. Sievier was an adventurer, libertine, litigant, former bankrupt, and inveterate gambler on cards and horses who lived by his wits.

As a two-year-old Sceptre won the July Stakes, but at the end of the season her trainer Charles Morton turned his yard into a private stable. Sievier therefore had to find a new trainer and his choice, born of invincible self-confidence, was himself – despite his total lack of experience.

He set up his base at Shrewton, Wiltshire, and decided that Sceptre should start her 1902 Classic campaign in the Lincoln. Even after her preparation for the big handicap had been ruined by his incompetent American assistant, she was beaten only a head.

She then easily brought off the Newmarket Classic double, disposing of male rivals in the 2,000 Guineas and strolling home in the 1,000 Guineas two days later.

She might well have justified even-money favouritism in the Derby, instead of finishing fourth behind Ard Patrick, but for an interrupted preparation and an injudicious ride by the inexperienced Bert Randall. Two days later she trounced her rivals in the Oaks.

**ONE FOR THE AGES:**
Sceptre was a supreme champion after winning four of the five Classics in 1902

**Foaled**
1899
**Pedigree**
Persimmon – Ornament
**Breeder**
1st Duke of Westminster
**Owners**
Bob Sievier and
William Bass
**Trainers**
Charles Morton, Bob
Sievier and Alec Taylor
**Main jockeys**
Bert Randall and
Fred Hardy
**Career record**
13 wins and eight places
from 25 runs
**Most famous for**
Winning four of the five
Classics in 1902 and
becoming the epitome
of female toughness
**Fate at stud**
Produced eight foals
including champion
filly Maid Of Corinth
and founded an
influential family

Formosa had won the same four in 1868, but only dead-heated in the 2,000 Guineas.

Sceptre lost half her 12 races in 1902, having been at the mercy of sub-standard jockeyship and the whims of a mercurial owner who finished the season as champion trainer but whose choice of races was dictated not by their suitability for her but by his desire for a successful gamble.

On the other hand, with a top trainer she would not have run in all five Classics and might now be no more famous than Formosa.

At the start of 1903 Sievier was in financial trouble, and after Sceptre's fifth place in the Lincoln he sold her for £25,000 to William Bass of the brewing family, who sent her to the great trainer Alec Taylor at Manton.

Thereafter she was campaigned in a more conventional fashion, although it took Taylor a while to realise how much work she needed. She won the Hardwicke Stakes but was still short of peak fitness in the 1903 Eclipse, in which the three principals won eight Classics between them.

In one of the candidates for the title 'Race of the Century', Ard Patrick and Sceptre fought a titanic duel, with the colt just prevailing by a neck. They outclassed the year-younger Rock Sand, who was en route to the Triple Crown.

Sceptre then trounced Rock Sand again in the Jockey Club Stakes, and also won the Duke of York Handicap at Kempton and the Champion Stakes. She failed to score as a five-year-old.

At stud she produced champion two-year-old filly Maid Of Corinth, and her long-term influence was profound. She died in 1926, aged 27.

Inevitably there were comparisons with Pretty Polly, who won the fillies' Triple Crown in 1904. Indeed, they won consecutive races at Newmarket on October 27, 1903, when Sceptre justified odds of 1-100 in the Limekiln Stakes and Pretty Polly took the Criterion Stakes. Pretty Polly was perhaps more brilliant, but Sceptre was inferior to none in toughness and charisma.

JOHN RANDALL

By this time Sievier had realised Sceptre was supremely tough and could stand an abnormal amount of work and racing. After further displays of incompetence by Randall in the Grand Prix de Paris and Coronation Stakes, he was replaced by Fred Hardy for victory in the St James's Palace Stakes, her fifth race in 16 days.

She then won the Nassau Stakes, and in the St Leger triumphed by three lengths to become the only horse to win four British Classics outright.

## "More than almost any other great champion she had her career influenced by the identity of her owner"

# 15
## DAHLIA

Refined and delicate, elegant and feminine, Dahlia was nobody's idea of a streetfighter when she first set foot on the track in 1972. What's more, this pioneering filly criss-crossed the Atlantic in an era when Secretariat ruled the roost on one side of the pond and Allez France waited for her on the other; yet she ended her career as one of the most revered racemares of all time with a distinguished career in the paddocks ahead of her.

Such was her brilliance and dominance that in 1974 she was simultaneously British Horse of the Year and holder of the Eclipse Award for Champion Turf Horse.

Her French trainer Maurice Zilber, risking a diplomatic incident in doing so, was moved to assert, after she had destroyed odds-on home favourite Tentam in the 1973 Washington DC International at Laurel Park, that "she could beat Secretariat any day in any country".

In the event, she never met Secretariat and never beat Allez France either, but the daughter of 1968 Arc winner Vaguely Noble nonetheless became the first mare to break the $1 million prize-money barrier.

The early 1970s were the playground of the Texas oil billionaires and Nelson Bunker Hunt, reckoned at one stage to have owned 1,000 racehorses, struck gold when he bred Dahlia, who after recording just one sprint win from four runs as a two-year-old, rapidly grew into an all-time great over middle distances.

For two seasons, the first foal of doughty US-bred mare Charming Alibi prowled the globe preying on lofty reputations, starting with that of dual Classic winner Mysterious in the 1974 Irish Oaks.

Having landed the Prix de la Grotte and Prix Saint-Alary in the early part of her three-year-old

**"Dahlia has to be one of the greatest ones for me"**

**Foaled**
March 25, 1970
**Pedigree**
Vaguely Noble –
Charming Alibi
**Breeder**
Nelson Bunker Hunt
**Owner**
Nelson Bunker Hunt
**Trainers**
Maurice Zilber and
Charlie Whittingham
**Main jockeys**
Bill Pyers and
Lester Piggott
**Career record**
15 wins and ten places
from 48 runs
**Most famous for**
Becoming the first horse
to win two King
Georges, proving top class on
two continents
**Fate at stud**
Of her 13 foals, 11 raced
and eight were winners,
including Group/Grade
1 scorers Dahar (1981,
by Lyphard) and Rivlia
(1982, by Riverman), with
her grandson Nedawi (out
of the Northern Dancer
mare Wajd) winning the
1998 St Leger

RIVALS TOILING: Dahlia
and Lester Piggott win the
Benson & Hedges Gold Cup
at York in August 1975

On her next start, the white-faced chestnut in the dark green and light green checks landed her first King George in course record time by six lengths, effortlessly flooring such exalted names as the colts Roberto and Rheingold. Apparently she ran only at the insistence of her trainer, who later revealed Hunt had threatened to remove all his horses from the yard if she were beaten. Zilber had barely a nervous moment.

"This was no defeat for the males," Tony Morris wrote in a contemporary piece in *Bloodstock Review*. "It was humiliation. They dictated the pace that destroyed them. They broke under the ferocious pressure. They were devoured by the filly."

In winning that November's DC International, she emulated Secretariat in thrashing the luckless Big Spruce. Although three wins at the top level was always going to be a hard act to follow the next year – a campaign that began with two further defeats by Allez France – she scaled new heights when she won the Grand Prix de Saint-Cloud under Yves Saint-Martin. Then she floored Highclere and Snow Knight to land her second King George, providing an armchair ride for Lester Piggott, who was back in the saddle for her first Benson and Hedges Gold Cup success at York.

Dahlia seemed to rely very little on her riders. "She did what she was supposed to do all by herself," said Ron Turcotte (also partner of Secretariat) after she had carried him to victory in Belmont's Man o' War Stakes, before Piggott was reunited with her for another track-record win, this time in the Canadian International at Woodbine.

"Dahlia has to be one of the greatest ones for me," said the Long Fellow of his nervy but rapier-like companion.

While 1975 proved less fruitful – yielding 'just' a repeat win in the B&H (beating Grundy) along with a third-placed bit part in the Grundy v Bustino King George – and a 1976 season in the care of Charlie Whittingham in California ended in defeat in the Las Palmas Handicap at Santa Anita (albeit after a glorious final Grade 1 in the Hollywood Invitational Handicap), the supermare's racing legacy was already assured.

She went on to become a first-class broodmare for Hunt until he sold her for $1.1m to Allen Paulson of Cigar fame, for whom she continued her breeding career until 1996, finally dying at the age of 31 and being buried at his Diamond A Farm in Kentucky.

PETER THOMAS

campaign, Dahlia had also twice been beaten by the mighty Allez France, which meant she lined up at the Curragh an 8-1 shot. But her three-length success under Australian Bill Pyers was the spectacular first step in her journey from gifted filly to living legend.

# 16
## ALL ALONG

All Along was a phenomenon, pure and simple. In her pomp she was a veritable racing machine, as she demonstrated in the autumn of 1983 when she won four Group/Grade 1 races within the space of 41 days.

Trained in France by Patrick Biancone, All Along was a plain, rangy filly with a masculine head and a heart-shaped blaze on her forehead. She first came to the attention of British racegoers when she contested the 1982 Oaks, although she disappointed in finishing sixth. Thereafter, she blossomed into a racehorse of uncommon power.

Later that season she landed the Prix Vermeille from Akiyda, who went on to win the Arc, before she

**VICTORY SALUTE:**
All Along and Walter Swinburn after winning the Prix de l'Arc de Triomphe in October 1983 – the first in a sequence of four Group/Grade 1 wins in the space of 41 days, which also included the Rothmans International, Turf Classic and Washington DC International

**Foaled**
April 17, 1979
**Pedigree**
Targowice – Agujita
**Breeder**
Dayton Ltd
**Owner**
Daniel Wildenstein
**Trainer**
Patrick Biancone
**Main jockey**
Walter Swinburn
**Career record**
Nine wins and six places
from 21 runs
**Most famous for**
Becoming the first
non-American-trained
runner to be voted US
Horse of the Year in 1983
**Fate at stud**
Dam of 13 foals, ten
runners and four winners,
among them Along All
(won Gr2 Prix Greffulhe)
and Arnaqueur (won
Listed race)

The Arc usually represents the culmination of a season's work but All Along was only just beginning. The opportunistic Biancone, then 31, had long had one eye on the $1 million bonus given to any horse who completed the North American Turf Triple. "The fact that there was this bonus for winning the triple was a big incentive," Biancone said at the time.

All Along made her bid in the year before the Breeders' Cup was inaugurated, when the Rothmans International at Woodbine, Turf Classic at Aqueduct and Washington DC International at Laurel Park were races of prime significance. All Along won them by a combined total of 14 lengths on rain-soaked tracks, to which Biancone maintained she was averse.

Little wonder, then, that Biancone christened her 'Cheval de Fer' – the Iron Horse. The fact no horse has ever won the Arc and Breeders' Cup Turf, which follows five weeks later, is attributed to the short timespan between them. All Along won four championship races in three different countries inside six weeks. "She was a filly who liked to go places," Biancone said. "She always enjoyed new surroundings."

Such unprecedented achievement gained All Along unprecedented recognition. In addition to becoming the first non-American-trained horse to be named US Horse of the Year, she was the first to win that accolade without having run on dirt. Racing fans in America were plainly in thrall to the Gallic galloping monster. She exuded an aura of invincibility.

Perhaps unsurprisingly, given her arduous exertions at four, All Along never rescaled the same heights in four starts the following season. She did finish third behind Sagace in the 1984 Arc, after which she returned to the US to chase home Lashkari in the inaugural Breeders' Cup Turf, which marked her racing swansong.

The prize-money she earned in the Turf propelled her to one more accolade as she became the highest-earning distaffer of all time. But her career in the paddocks proved disappointing: she bred a solitary Group-race winner from 13 live foals.

All Along died in 2005 in Kentucky, aged 26, two years after she had been retired. Wildenstein's son, Alec, summed it up succinctly when he said on her passing: "All Along took us on a joyride like no other, culminating in an achievement we scarcely dared dream about, which was horse of the year in America."
**JULIAN MUSCAT**

## "She was a filly who liked to go places. She always enjoyed new surroundings"

succumbed by a scant neck after a prolonged stretch duel with Half Iced in the Japan Cup. This was an era when international racing really took hold, and in All Along connections had a tough and durable filly who thrived on long-distance travel.

As a four-year-old, she made three unsuccessful starts ahead of the 1983 Prix de l'Arc de Triomphe. So much so that Lester Piggott, booked by Biancone in the build-up, jumped ship to ride Awaasif. Come the big day and Piggott, who finished 13th, would have had a distant view of All Along's rear end as the 17-1 shot, ridden by Walter Swinburn, passed most of her 25 opponents down the Longchamp straight to beat Sun Princess by a length.

# 17
## ZENYATTA

When all is said and done, it was only a head. But for that agonising margin, the distance by which the great Zenyatta – the wonderful, incomparable, scarcely believable Zenyatta – failed to nail the aptly named Blame on her final start, then the sweet-natured she-hulk with the puppy-dog temperament would have ended her career with a totally unblemished record.

In the event, she forfeited her unbeaten status on her 20th start as the Breeders' Cup Classic of 2010 produced a fittingly dramatic conclusion to an unforgettable racing life under the floodlights at Churchill Downs. Then again, she had already won a place among racing's immortals, long since transcending the sport in which she established a modern-day North American record with her 19-race winning streak in unrestricted races, among them 13 Grade 1s.

Her every move followed by a legion of ardently devoted fans, Zenyatta was charisma made bulging equine flesh, blessed with an irresistible talent yet soft as a kitten at the same time. Bought for $60,000 as a yearling at the Keeneland September Sale in 2005, she was named after The Police's third LP, Zenyatta Mondatta; her owner Jerry Moss had signed the faux-reggae titans to his record label A&M.

Sent to her owner's farm in Florida, she was such a gross horse that she did not race until the autumn of her three-year-old career. "She covered the ground and came with rave reviews," recalled trainer John Shirreffs. "But then you didn't know if she just had a big stride or if she had any speed to go with it. We just had to wait for her to put it all together."

Once she did, though, she was something to behold, winning a string of top races, more often than not in utterly thrilling come-from-behind fashion. Zenyatta's version of *The Late Late Show* be-

> **"You can tell when she puts in gear – she lowers her head, pauses and goes vroom"**

ONE MORE GO: Zenyatta at Churchill Downs three days before the final start of her career in the Breeders' Cup Classic. She was beaten a head by Blame – the only defeat she suffered in 20 races

her home state during an era when synthetic surfaces prevailed in California. For such detractors, humble pie was on the menu when she recorded her 14th straight victory in a stunning display on the Pro-Ride in the 2009 Breeders' Cup Classic at Santa Anita, where she had won the Ladies' Classic (now Distaff) the year before. Zenyatta naturally missed the break and ambled around ten lengths and more off the lead on the backstretch before circling the entire field to totally overwhelm her rivals.

Cue unbridled adulation in the Santa Anita stands. "There are times when you look and you say, 'Boy, can she get there?'" marvelled Shirreffs. "But you can tell when she puts in gear – she lowers her head, pauses, and goes vroom."

Despite her estimable record, Zenyatta lost out in the Horse of the Year ballot to the three-year-old Rachel Alexandra, who had compiled her own flawless campaign on the east coast. They never met, even though Zenyatta was kept in training as a six-year-old in 2010, when she won five more Grade 1s before heading to Churchill Downs for the Classic and only the second run of her life on a dirt surface.

Mike Smith let her lope along seven lengths adrift of the remainder, even further behind than she usually was; the magnificent mare duly unleashed her customary late charge down the stretch, where her jockey unleashed his own volley of unedifying whip cracks in a desperate bid to thwart Blame, a well-ridden Grade 1 performer with home-track advantage.

Zenyatta was in front two strides after the wire, of course, but it was two strides too late. Imagine if Black Caviar hadn't actually won at Royal Ascot after Luke Nolen dropped his hands and you're getting the picture. But such an unwelcome result did not prevent the crowd's showering of the runner-up with their post-race cheers as the victorious Blame left the track almost unnoticed. It might not have been fair but it was understandable: he might not have shot Bambi's mother but it would not have been a surprise if police had asked him to help with their enquiries.

That Zenyatta failed at the last – so narrowly, in adverse circumstances, under a questionable ride – should not really be held against her, and it did not hurt her at the Horse of the Year vote, which she finally won by a landslide. "I always tell people God made a very special horse when he created Zenyatta," suggested Shirreffs. No quibbling here.
NICHOLAS GODFREY

**Foaled**
April 1, 2004
**Pedigree**
Street Cry – Vertigineux
**Breeder**
Maverick Production Limited
**Owners**
Jerry and Ann Moss
**Trainer**
John Shirreffs
**Main jockey**
Mike Smith
**Career record**
19 wins from 20 runs
**Most famous for**
Her unbeaten run – often grabbing victory from a seemingly impossible position with her customary late charge – and that one agonising defeat
**Fate at stud**
Retired to Lane's End in Kentucky. Has produced foals by Bernardini and Tapit (Cozmic One and Ziconic – neither has shown much) before twice being bred to War Front; both foals died (one after a paddock accident, the second after just two days owing to complications). She was bred to Medaglia D'Oro in 2016

came one of the hottest tickets in the racing world; she was featured on the TV show *60 Minutes*; she was profiled in Oprah Winfrey's magazine. She was a drama queen at heart – witness the prancing and dancing in the parade ring before her races that became one of many Zenyatta trademarks – and loved all the attention she habitually received.

Yet there were also non-believers who considered her a plastic-track princess as she rarely left

# 18

# BOSRA SHAM

Henry Cecil had a way with the ladies, although few taxed the master of Warren Place to a greater degree than Bosra Sham. The filly blessed by abundant natural ability also came with the most delicate of hooves.

Cecil's 11th-hour scares with Bosra Sham's near-fore were a familiar refrain throughout their relationship. The trainer became immensely fond of the chestnut with a pair of white hind legs that made her look like she was clad in surgical stockings. But it was she who wielded the scalpel as she carved up an array of talented older males in her all too brief career.

Those problematic hooves aside, Bosra Sham was a gorgeous physical specimen who fetched 530,000 guineas at auction. She was the most expensive yearling bought in Europe in 1994, and was something of a bargain. Her prowess was such that she was sent off odds-on in eight of her ten career starts.

That included her debut, which she won with ease before she again started odds-on when winning the Group 1 Fillies' Mile by three and a half lengths. She had already been obliged to miss the May Hill Stakes in between with a sore foot and the same condition forced her to miss her final gallop before the 1996 1,000 Guineas.

"It was touch and go whether she could run," recalls Tim Bulwer-Long, racing manager to Bosra Sham's owner Wafic Said. "We knew she wouldn't be at her best but Henry felt she would still be good enough."

So it proved, although Bosra Sham was demonstrably sore in the winner's circle after landing the fillies' Classic by a length and a half. The wall of her near-fore hoof was prone to breaking up when she was shod, even in plastic shoes; so much so she required nearly five months' rest before she lined up against Mark Of Esteem in the Queen Elizabeth II Stakes.

"Expectations were high based on her homework," Bulwer-Long says. "In the end it ended in disappointment but Bosra Sham hadn't run for four months.

"Perhaps that told, although Mark Of Esteem did win very well."

The QEII served to bring Bosra Sham on, so that Cecil was confident ahead of her assignment against Halling in the Champion Stakes. Halling had established himself as Europe's pre-eminent performer over a mile and a quarter. He started at evens yet Bosra Sham, under Pat Eddery, stalked the favourite before streaking away to win by two and a half lengths.

"That was a great day," Bulwer-Long says. "What wasn't that well known was that Henry had had further problems with her foot the night before the race. He had to remove her shoe and have her replated in the morning."

That display earned Bosra Sham the highest rating of any horse in Europe and North America over a mile and a quarter on the 1996 International Classifications. And she was almost as impressive when sauntering to an eight-length triumph in the Prince of Wales's Stakes at Royal Ascot the following season, after which the wheels – or in her case hooves – fell off.

Kieren Fallon was heavily criticised when Bosra Sham finished only third at 4-7 in the Eclipse Stakes. And with Eddery recalled for the International Stakes, Bosra Sham lost a shoe when rounding the home turn before she limped home in fourth place, never to be seen again.

But for her brittle feet, Cecil was adamant Bosra Sham would have been a dominant distaffer. She showed as much when brushing Halling aside in the Champion Stakes in the defining performance of her career. On that day she outclassed a horse who had been beaten just twice in his previous 14 starts – both times on dirt.

JULIAN MUSCAT

**Foaled**
February 28, 1993
**Pedigree**
Woodman – Korveya
**Breeder**
Gerald Leigh
**Owner**
Wafic Said
**Trainer**
Henry Cecil
**Main jockeys**
Kieren Fallon and
Pat Eddery
**Career record**
Seven wins and two
places from ten runs
**Most famous for**
Contemptuous dismissal
of dual Eclipse and dual
International Stakes
winner Halling in the
1996 Champion Stakes
**Fate at stud**
Dam of five foals to race
and two winners, among
them Rosberg, winner
of a Grade 3 in Canada

> **"Her prowess was such that she was sent off odds-on in eight of her ten career starts"**

WINNING PAT: Bosra Sham and her lad John Scott in the winner's enclosure at Royal Ascot after the 1997 Prince of Wales's Stakes. Trainer Henry Cecil is in the background

NEWMARKET STROLL:
Bosra Sham and Pat Eddery
win the 1,000 Guineas in
1996 by a length and a half
from Matiya (pink cap)

# 19

# NOBLESSE

Paddy Prendergast was a pioneering figure on the Irish racing scene. Having started his training career in County Kildare during World War II, the former jump jockey began to mount regular raids on major British two-year-old races in the early 1950s.

The brilliant Windy City led the way with victory in the Gimcrack in 1951. Two years later The Pie King became the first of the trainer's six Coventry Stakes winners. By the end of the decade Prendergast had won races such as the Champagne Stakes, the Cheveley Park, the Lowther, the Norfolk, the Queen Mary and the Richmond Stakes.

In 1960 he saddled Martial to become the first Irish-trained winner of the 2,000 Guineas. In the same year came the foaling of a filly – sold in utero by Stanhope Joel – by Mossborough, the sire of Vincent O'Brien's 1958 Arc winner Ballymoss, out of Duke's Delight.

Bought as a yearling for 4,200 guineas by the Anglo-Irish Bloodstock Agency, Noblesse was sent into training with Prendergast to carry the colours of Evelyn Olin, second wife of John Merrill Olin, an Illinois-born chemical engineer and inventor who specialised in the design and manufacture of arms and ammunition.

A member of a juvenile team that included the Molecomb winner Royal Indiscretion and Whistling Wind, who won the National Breeders' Produce Stakes at Sandown, Noblesse had established a significant reputation on the Curragh gallops prior to her debut in the Blue Seal Stakes.

After she won that Ascot event by a comfortable five lengths, Prendergast was sufficiently encouraged to send her back to England to take on the colts in the Timeform Gold Cup, inaugurated the previous year at the instigation of Phil Bull as Europe's richest two-year-old race.

Ridden by the Australian Garnie Bougoure, Ireland's champion jockey in 1960, she won readily by three lengths. She remains the only filly to have won the race now known as the Racing Post Trophy.

On the strength of just two races, Noblesse was named champion British and Irish juvenile filly. Following a bad winter and cold spring, Prendergast did not have time to prepare her for the 1,000 Guineas. Instead, she made a winning seasonal debut in the third running of the Musidora Stakes at York, accounting for Partholon and the Royal Lodge winner Star Moss in smooth fashion.

Returning for the Oaks, she was sent off the 4-11 favourite. Always going well, she accelerated when asked by Bougoure a furlong out to win by ten lengths from the 1,000 Guineas runner-up Spree. Bougoure claimed she could have doubled the margin and several experienced observers suggested her performance was good enough to have beaten the brilliant Relko in the 1963 Derby.

A minor hock injury forced Noblesse to miss the King George and in her place Prendergast sent over Irish Derby winner Ragusa, who proved an able deputy, beating 1961 Timeform Gold Cup winner Miralgo.

The Arc was now the target for the filly, who returned to action in the Prix Vermeille with Lester Piggott aboard. Failing to find anything like the blistering acceleration she had shown in her previous races, she managed only third. She was found to be lame and was retired.

Timeform described the 133-rated champion three-year-old filly in glowing terms: "In the first four of her races she hardly needed to gallop seriously for more than fifty yards, and yet she won all of them by a wide margin, and her turn of foot was something to marvel at."

She was perhaps the best filly ever trained in Ireland, although Irish racegoers never got an opportunity to see her in action.

ALAN SWEETMAN

**Foaled**
1960
**Pedigree**
Mossborough – Duke's Delight
**Breeder**
PM Margetts
**Owner**
Evelyn Olin
**Trainer**
Paddy Prendergast
**Main jockey**
Garnie Bougoure
**Career record**
Four wins and one place from five runs
**Most famous for**
Winning the 1963 Oaks by ten lengths
**Fate at stud**
Five foals, all winners, including Where You Lead, an influential broodmare

**"In the first four of her races she hardly needed to gallop seriously for more than fifty yards, and yet she won all of them by a wide margin"**

ON PARADE: Noblesse was sent off the 4-11 favourite for the Oaks in 1963 and ran out a ten-length winner

# 20

# OH SO SHARP

While some racing terminology is a bit old-fashioned it can be beautifully descriptive and Timeform's succinct seven-word summation of Oh So Sharp – "a grand mover with a raking stride" – nails the majesty of the great mare.

Along with Meld (1955), Oh So Sharp is one of just two winners of the fillies' Triple Crown since the Second World War having landed the 1,000 Guineas, Oaks and St Leger for Sheikh Mohammed and Henry Cecil.

She was a daughter of the brilliant Kris, winner of 14 of his 16 races, who was bred by Lord Howard de Walden, whose genial outlook on life may have been shaped by the fact that he inherited just under 100 acres of the West End.

As a student in the 1930s, de Walden was driving in Munich when he knocked down a pedestrian who sadly escaped with only the most insignificant injuries. If only he had floored it and done the job properly. It was Adolf Hitler.

But we will leave the Führer and return to the filly. Oh So Sharp was unbeaten in her three races at two, winning her maiden under Paul Eddery followed by the Solario Stakes – more prestigious than nowadays – and the Fillies' Mile.

And she had a way about her – an enthusiasm – that marked her out. She looked to relish the job.

Oh So Sharp was also in the hands of a man to whom fillies were second nature. She won the Nell Gwyn comfortably and was sent off 2-1 favourite in the 1,000 Guineas with Steve Cauthen, gentleman of the turf, on board.

But it was far from plain sailing. In the Dip, Cauthen looked in trouble and had to give it everything as Bella Colora and Al Bahathri – two rattling good fillies – went for home.

Coming out of the Dip, Oh So Sharp gave everything and finished really strongly to get up at the death. It was a vintage Guineas in calibre and spectacle as Oh So Sharp beat Al Bahathri by a short head with Bella Colora another short head back in third.

Cauthen has always been adamant Oh So Sharp was the best filly he rode but reflecting years later admitted that "we barely got there".

She was all quality but it was stamina as much as anything that won the day.

So well was Oh So Sharp working at home in the run-up to Epsom there was talk of running her in the Derby. In fact Cecil and Cauthen won the Derby with Slip Anchor in the apricot silks of de Walden.

Oh So Sharp started 6-4 favourite for the Oaks and hosed up. Always handy, she led two out and powered away to win by six lengths in a fast time from the redoubtable Triptych.

The plan had been to go for the Nassau next but when Slip Anchor met with a setback, Oh So Sharp was rerouted to the King George and, a public favourite by now, was sent off odds-on.

She led early in the straight but was mugged close home and beaten a neck by the Dick Hern-trained Petoski, on whom Willie Carson produced a tactical triumph of timing and sheer strength.

Oh So Sharp then went to York for the Benson and Hedges Gold Cup. Again she was beaten but there was a good reason: Lester Piggott. Riding Commanche Run, he set a rather lackadaisical pace and then turned the volume up three furlongs out. The pursuers could never lay a glove on the pair and Oh So Sharp was beaten three-quarters of a length.

And so to Town Moor for the fillies' Triple Crown. Oh So Sharp made hard work of it and was nothing like the majestic filly of Oaks day. She ground it out to win by three-quarters of a length and a head from Phardante and Lanfranco. It was Cecil's triumph and he admitted: "Another week and it might have been too late. She was beginning to go and I was just hanging on to her."

As only he could have done. It was Cecil's Triple Crown as much as Oh So Sharp's.

ALASTAIR DOWN

> ## "She had a way about her – an enthusiasm – that marked her out. She looked to relish the job"

**Foaled**
March 30, 1982
**Pedigree**
Kris – Oh So Fair
**Breeder**
Sheikh Mohammed
**Owner**
Sheikh Mohammed
**Trainer**
Henry Cecil
**Main jockey**
Steve Cauthen
**Career record**
Seven wins and two seconds from nine runs
**Most famous for**
Becoming only the second winner of the fillies' Triple Crown
**Fate at stud**
Produced winner of Group 1 Prix Saint-Alary and Grade 2 winners in US. Also the granddam of 2012 Tasmanian Derby winner Methuselah

PRIDE AND JOY: owner Sheikh Mohammed with Oh So Sharp after his star filly had landed the 1985 Oaks – the second leg of her Triple Crown – by six lengths from the redoubtable Triptych

OH SO SHARP

IT'S A THRILLER:
Oh So Sharp's powerful
late surge denies
Al Bahathri (centre) and
Bella Colora (far side)
in the 1985 1,000
Guineas at Newmarket

# 21

# INDIAN SKIMMER

One of the abiding memories of Indian Skimmer is not of her striding out through the final furlong on the way to big-race success, but of her standing stock still on the Rowley Mile on a misty autumn afternoon, declining to canter to post before the Champion Stakes.

Indian Skimmer could be, in the words of her trainer Henry Cecil, a cowbag. On this occasion she was ably demonstrating that faculty, and it wasn't until Cecil himself came out to indulgently remonstrate with her that she consented to move. They walked a little way down the course together, Cecil not minding about the ruination of his Gucci loafers, Indian Skimmer not minding that she'd been coaxed into participating in the silly race after all. A few minutes later she came back alone, her rivals lost in the fog, the race won, the immovable object transformed into the irresistible force.

"I have trained some very good animals but she is brilliant," said Cecil, in a very rare example of bias. "It would be unfair to her not to say she is the best I have ever had – and that includes the colts."

In 1987, arguably Cecil's most complete season of domination, Indian Skimmer flashed across the European landscape like a sleek grey comet, carrying all before her. She began her five-race winning streak in April at Wolverhampton – something that few champions can boast – and stretched it unto the Prix de Diane at Chantilly in June, when she became the first horse to beat the outstanding Miesque.

A mile and a quarter was emphatically not Miesque's best trip but Indian Skimmer had her cold at a mile, tucking in behind her pacemaker until exploding away under Steve Cauthen at the two-furlong pole. She swiftly drew four lengths clear, looking the very image of elegance in her dappled coat, the chic-est thing around on French racing's chic-est afternoon.

A back problem put her conquering career on hold, and when she returned at four it took a little time to locate her former brilliance, but by September she had it under lock and key again. By now a little paler, and ridden by Michael Roberts, she reversed the form of the International Stakes by keeping on too strongly for Shady Heights in the Irish Champion Stakes at Phoenix Park, doled out a lesson to the sorority when cantering to Sun Chariot Stakes success, and crowned the year in that aforementioned Champion Stakes when stamping her class – and her temperament

PROUD OWNER:
Sheikh Mohammed with Indian Skimmer after the 1987 Prix de Diane at Chantilly when she became the first filly to beat the outstanding French star Miesque. In the background Steve Cauthen debriefs Henry Cecil

**Foaled**
February 12, 1984
**Pedigree**
Storm Bird – Nobiliare
**Breeders**
Ashford Stud and
Ronald Worswick
**Owner**
Sheikh Mohammed
**Trainer**
Henry Cecil
**Main jockey**
Steve Cauthen
**Career record**
Ten wins and four places
from 16 runs
**Most famous for**
Charismatic champion
and one of the best fillies
trained by the master;
beautiful grey coat
**Fate at stud**
Only foal to race was a
minor winner; granddam
of South African
champion Ipi Tombe

– in unforgettable fashion, ghosting gloriously out of the gloom to beat Persian Heights by four lengths.

There was an aura of glamour around Indian Skimmer that made her every appearance exciting. She had her problems at home – Cecil described her as a 'cripple' – but when she went racing her winning combination of looks and talent commandeered the attention like a film star. On her day – and there were many – she was capable of electrifying brilliance, and defeat – such as in the Breeders' Cup Turf, a race too far on more than one level – was easy to make allowances for.

She bounced back at five, was reunited with Cauthen, showed her old panache in the Prix d'Ispahan, and then went to Sandown for an Eclipse that was gleefully billed as 'the race of the century',

**"I have trained some very good animals but she is brilliant"**

with dual Classic winner Nashwan and crack miler Warning in opposition. It was not the race of the century – the unrelenting pace set by her pacemaker Opening Verse meant that neither Indian Skimmer nor Warning could make any impression on the contest. Nashwan prevailed, but Indian Skimmer was unable even to pass Opening Verse for second place.

It was the last we saw of her, and not the farewell we'd wished for. Cecil would later have to redraw Indian Skimmer's 'best-ever' label owing to the exploits of the incomparable Frankel, but the old cowbag never strayed far from his heart. She must have liked him too; perhaps we'll leave them there, walking away into the mist together, another Group 1 win just minutes away.
STEVE DENNIS

SITTING PRETTY:
Indian Skimmer and
Steve Cauthen stride
to an authoritative success
in the Musidora Stakes
at York in May 1987

# 22
# MINDING

A quirk of fate has denied Minding the undisputed mantle of being recognised as the best filly to emerge from Ballydoyle during either of its two extraordinary tenancies.

Aidan O'Brien spent a long time waiting for a filly who could compete with and beat the colts in Group 1 company – then two came along at once. In fairness to Found, whose Racing Post Rating of 124 and official rating of 123 are both a pound higher than Minding's respective marks, she was here first.

Whereas Found managed to win the Prix de l'Arc de Triomphe before reaching the clubhouse, injury intervened before Minding embarked on the back nine.

Minding began instead her four-year-old career with an effortless reappearance win in the Group 2 Mooresbridge Stakes in May 2017, after which she sustained a pastern injury, which ultimately ended her career.

Just like Found claimed the scalp of 2015 Derby hero Golden Horn at the zenith of her Classic campaign, Minding emulated that stellar feat by stamping her authority all over the QEII field at Ascot in 2016 when reverting to a mile for the first time in five starts across as many months.

Heavily backed, the exceptional daughter of Galileo swept to the front over a furlong out courtesy of a searing turn of foot under Ryan Moore.

Victory against the colts in open company constituted an emphatic illustration of Minding's ex-

> **"She has lots of pace and masses of talent"**

alted status, with the winners of both the 2,000 Guineas and its Irish equivalent, Galileo Gold and Awtaad, among her victims.

Of course, if the presence of a particular stable-mate meant for one quirk of fate that had a slightly negative consequence for Minding, the absence of an unidentified other contributed to a positive outcome. In short, last year O'Brien lacked the sort of marquee colt that might have usually denied Minding her place in the QEII.

Still, that merely presented this outstandingly robust individual with an opportunity to become the first filly in 29 years to win the race. It was what she did with her chance that will ultimately leave an enduring mark, a glorious legacy that she was already on her way to moulding.

"To stay a mile and a half and then do that over a mile, they have to be very special," gushed an admiring O'Brien. "She was too good for them, too strong. She has lots of pace and masses of talent. To beat the colts is unbelievable – she is an incredible filly."

Successful in both the Moyglare Stud Stakes and Fillies' Mile as a juvenile, Minding returned with a

**IN SPLENDID ISOLATION:** Minding and Ryan Moore in front of the stands after winning the Queen Elizabeth II Stakes at Ascot in October 2016

stylish 1,000 Guineas triumph at Newmarket, where she spearheaded a stunning 1-2-3 for O'Brien.

In the Irish 1,000 Guineas three weeks later, having smacked her head leaving the stalls, she was narrowly foiled on soft ground by the mud-loving Jet Setting. Punters, though, were undeterred, again sending her off at odds-on for the Oaks less than a fortnight later.

At Epsom, Minding defied the step up to a mile and a half with an exquisite turn of foot, before then dropping back to a mile and a quarter to land both the Pretty Polly and Nassau Stakes.

First pitted against the colts in what was a memorable edition of the Irish Champion Stakes, she lost little in defeat at Leopardstown when outpointed by Almanzor and Found.

Then she seized her moment in spectacular fashion, her QEII coup a fitting denouement to a superlative campaign. In accruing seven Group 1s, Minding is already the most prolific top-level filly O'Brien has trained.

She went into retirement with the accolade of being described by O'Brien as "one of the best fillies I have ever trained". **RICHARD FORRISTAL**

**Foaled**
February 10, 2013
**Pedigree**
Galileo – Lillie Langtry
**Breeders**
Orpendale, Chelston and Wynatt
**Owners**
Derrick Smith, Sue Magnier and Michael Tabor
**Trainer**
Aidan O'Brien
**Main jockey**
Ryan Moore
**Career record**
Nine wins and four places from 13 runs
**Most famous for**
The quality and versatility that enabled her to become the first filly to win the QEII since 1987

SPECIAL FILLY: Minding and Ryan Moore draw away from their rivals to win the 2016 Oaks at Epsom

CLOSE UP: Ryan Moore and Minding land the Nassau Stakes at Glorious Goodwood in July 2016

# 23

# PERSONAL ENSIGN

It was a cold and miserable afternoon at Churchill Downs on the day Personal Ensign made history. Rain had turned the main track beneath the iconic Twin Spires into a mucky quagmire she didn't like, and she was slip-slidin' away all over the slop as Kentucky Derby-winning filly Winning Colors established an eight-length advantage over her as they went into the far turn.

What followed was extraordinary, an almost unbearably dramatic come-from-behind victory that has entered the annals of US racing.

Personal Ensign had been trapped in tight quarters and was still four lengths down at the furlong marker but was closing relentlessly.

Legendary commentator Tom Durkin made the call: "Here comes Personal Ensign unleashing a furious run."

But time was running out and the wire looked sure to win. It didn't, although Personal Ensign needed every ounce of her courage and every inch

PERFECT 13: Personal Ensign (left) ends her career with an extraordinary come-from-behind victory in the 1988 Breeders' Cup Distaff

**Foaled**
April 27, 1984
**Pedigree**
Private Account –
Grecian Banner
**Breeder**
Ogden Phipps
**Owner**
Ogden Phipps
**Trainer**
Claude R (Shug)
McGaughey
**Main jockey**
Randy Romero
**Career record**
13 wins from 13 runs
**Most famous for**
Unbeaten in perfect
career, climaxing in a
nerve-shredding victory
over Winning Colors in
Breeders' Cup Distaff as
a four-year-old in 1988
**Stud record**
Enjoyed very successful
broodmare career
(dam of Grade 1 winners
Miner's Mark, My Flag
and Traditionally); died of
natural causes after being
pensioned at Claiborne
on April 8, 2010

But disaster was to follow as she broke down prior to the Breeders' Cup Juvenile Fillies, breaking her near-hind leg in two places. "We never thought she'd race again," recalled McGaughey.

Against the odds, though, and with five screws inserted into her leg, Personal Ensign was to make a miraculous recovery, the remainder of her career a veritable triumph over adversity.

Although she did not reappear for 11 months, nothing could lay a glove on her in four runs during a five-week period in the autumn of her three-year-old season, all of them at Belmont and all of them won by daylight for a combined total of more than 18 lengths, ending in the Grade 1 Beldame.

"If she gets in trouble, she's so fast she can get out of it," said jockey Randy Romero.

She missed the Breeders' Cup again, her connections reasoning it might have been a step too far after running so frequently in such a short period of time. No matter, because she was to be kept busy at four, making up for lost time in a winning spree taking in a litany of top races in the New York/New Jersey area.

Personal Ensign won six races before the Breeders' Cup, five of them Grade 1 affairs, establishing total domination over her own sex in claiming the Shuvee, Hempstead (by seven), Molly Pitcher (by eight), Maskette and Beldame (by five and a half). She also beat males in the Whitney, overcoming champion sprinter Gulch.

All that remained was a last hurrah with her first visit to the Breeders' Cup as she attempted to complete a perfect career with her 13th consecutive victory.

If the weather did not turn up, then her rivals did, notably Winning Colors, who loved setting the pace and loved the muddy racetrack. The Personal Ensign team almost gave up the ghost.

"She wasn't handling the track that day – she just couldn't get a hold of it," reported Romero.

"Not today, she's beaten," muttered McGaughey according to contemporary reports as three-time Grade 1 winner Goodbye Halo veered out into her path in the late stretch. But Personal Ensign did not know how to get beaten: she bore down on Winning Colors, getting home by a desperate nostril on the final start of an amazing career.

A productive life as a broodmare was to follow and Personal Ensign is also remembered in a Grade 1 event at Saratoga in August. In a sense, though, they need not have bothered. No-one is going to forget about her in a hurry, that's for sure.
NICHOLAS GODFREY

of the stretch to claim Winning Colors. The margin, unsurprisingly, was the smallest available – a celebrated unbeaten record had been preserved at the end of a truly remarkable career by a nose.

The four-year-old had won every one of her 13 races, eight of them in Grade 1 company. She was the first top-level performer since Colin went 15 for 15 in the early 1900s to retire with a perfect record.

An enduring place in the record books looked a long way away at the end of Personal Ensign's two-year-old campaign.

True, she was regally bred and exquisitely well connected as part of the resurgent Phipps dynasty conditioned by their private trainer Shug McGaughey. She also looked a filly of rare distinction from the get-go, carrying the famous black and cherry red silks to a narrow Grade 1 success in the Frizette after a runaway near-13-length victory on debut at the same venue.

**"If she gets in trouble, she's so fast she can get out of it"**

# 24

# ALLEZ FRANCE

There are horses who capture the racing fan in all of us but, while we might not care to admit it, very few break through to the wider public consciousness.

To understand the appeal of Allez France, you have to go beyond her startling record of eight Group 1 successes across four seasons and her towering Timeform Rating of 136; beyond even her role as the best-ever racehorse to be sired by French champion Sea-Bird.

Allez France became a national darling when mass media exposure of racing was being driven by the popularity of the Tierce bet, making her jockey Yves Saint-Martin a cover star for *Paris-Match* as well as *Paris-Turf*.

Allez France was bought privately as a yearling for $160,000 by art dealer Daniel Wildenstein – another great figure of the era, Nelson Bunker Hunt, reportedly turned the filly down on account of his distaste for Sea-Bird as a sire – and sent to Chantilly, where trainer Albert Klimscha produced her to win what is now the Prix Marcel Boussac on only her second start at two.

At three she became the first filly to land the Poule d'Essai des Pouliches, Prix de Diane and Prix Vermeille since 1948.

A measure of the shock at her defeat in the 1973 Arc is that the headline 'Rheingold beats Allez France' shared the front page of the following day's *Le Parisien Libéré* newspaper with the death of racing driver François Cevert, relegating news of the Yom Kippur War to the inside pages.

"When we got to the Arc I knew Rheingold very well, having won the Grand Prix de Saint-Cloud on him," says Saint-Martin. "He'd been second in the Epsom Derby and was obviously a very good horse. I think perhaps Allez France was maybe slightly

below her best that day and, on very soft ground, 2,400 metres [a mile and a half] probably stretched her stamina a bit. But she was beaten fair and square, there were no excuses."

With Klimscha retiring, it was Argentine expatriate trainer Angel Penna (below, with Allez France) who guided her on an unbeaten streak of four successes in 1974 that included the Prix Ganay, in which she dispatched her great rival Dahlia for a sixth time.

Allez France tuned up in the Prix Foy but the country was made to hold its collective breath when Saint-Martin broke a bone after being thrown in the paddock at Maisons-Laffitte just ten days before the Arc, leading Wildenstein and Penna to contact Lester Piggott.

"Normally I would have been out for three weeks," says Saint-Martin. "I found a surgeon who was a hip specialist and I went to his clinic for treatment. I did special exercises in the pool every day and had

MY GIRL: Allez France with trainer Angel Penna after winning the 1974 Prix de l'Arc de Triomphe at Longchamp

electronic massage. On the Friday morning I had an injection of Novocaine in the hip and then rode out for an hour and a half. I rode without the injection on Saturday and then Sunday I went racing."

France Television gave an eight-minute segment of its hour-long current affairs show on the eve of the race, during which Wildenstein's son Guy assured celebrated racing journalist Leon Zitrone and the viewing millions that the love story between Yves Saint-Martin and Allez France was set to continue.

In the race itself, having saved ground around the inner, Saint-Martin appeared in the perfect spot but when the gap appeared early in the straight Allez France took the decision out of her rider's hands.

---

## "Perhaps runner-up Comtesse Du Loire came at us a little late and the post saved us"

Saint-Martin says: "It was a risk to ride so soon after the injury but she took a lot of knowing. The trip [2,400 metres] was as far as she could go and I was at the limit. It was a difficult job because she began too well and I had to leave her quietly to just tick away during the race. Then she saw daylight too early. Perhaps runner-up Comtesse Du Loire came at us a little late and the post saved me."

Allez France stayed in training at five but, despite adding a second Ganay, was never quite able to rekindle her very best form, finishing fifth in the Arc before adding a second runner-up spot in Newmarket's Champion Stakes to the one she collected in 1973.

A solitary attempt on dirt in the US added to the impression Allez France was a homebird and may contribute to the feeling in Britain and elsewhere that her contemporary, dual King George winner Dahlia, was at least her equal. But to her adoring public at home, there really was only one queen of Longchamp.
SCOTT BURTON

**Foaled**
May 24, 1970
**Pedigree**
Sea-Bird – Priceless Gem
**Breeder**
Bieber-Jacobs Stable
**Owner**
Daniel Wildenstein
**Trainers**
Albert Klimscha and Angel Penna
**Main jockey**
Yves Saint-Martin
**Career record**
13 wins from 21 runs
**Most famous for**
Cementing her reputation as one of France's all-time greats when landing the 1974 Prix de l'Arc de Triomphe for an expectant nation
**Fate at stud**
Produced two winners from her four foals to reach the track. The Seattle Slew colt Air De France won once and went on to sire 12 stakes winners in Australia, while her daughter by Nureyev, Action Francaise, landed the G3 Prix de Sandringham

# 25

# SUN PRINCESS

Twelve lengths is a wide and impressive margin of victory in any race. In a Classic, it's practically off the scale of surprise and awe. Those were the emotions provoked at Epsom by Sun Princess, who was a superlative filly despite the character flaw that threatened to derail her brilliant career.

"Sometimes I wonder how good she could have been if she'd been more tractable," says jockey Willie Carson. "All she wanted to do was gallop, go flat out. She was very, very good but a tricky filly to ride."

Notably headstrong as a two-year-old, Sun Princess had just one run over an inadequate trip, where the foremost concern was to teach her to race with restraint rather than simply high-tailing it for the horizon. She finished runner-up, as she did on her reappearance at three in that informative Listed race at Newbury over a mile and a quarter, in which kindness was again the watchword. She was beaten by Ski Sailing, whose rider Steve Cauthen warmed to his filly's Oaks potential.

"Steve said 'I'm going to win the Oaks', and I just said to him 'I'm sorry, but you aren't'," chuckles Carson. "We had a £100 bet between us. Lester Piggott overheard us, and a little later he sidled up to me and said 'I'd like a bit of that bet, y'know'."

The Oaks is a great race; in 1983 it wasn't a race, it was a parade, an exhibition. Sun Princess allowed Carson to be a jockey for the first six furlongs and then took matters into her own hands, assuming command of a Classic like few horses before or since. On the way down the hill she pulled her way to the front, anticipating that startling mid-race move from Arazi in the Breeders' Cup but with all the refined elegance you'd expect from a Ballymacoll-raised, Dick Hern-trained filly.

"Could I keep her under restraint?" comes the rhetorical question. "Five furlongs from home my arms were so tired I couldn't hold on to her any longer. I didn't send her on, she just took me there."

Sun Princess, a two-race maiden, simply ran away from the field, extending her lead with every stride. Behind her, like rowing boats bobbing in a speedboat's wake, were future Champion Stakes winner Cormorant Wood, Breeders' Cup winner Royal Heroine and Nassau Stakes winner Acclimatise, but Sun Princess thrashed them. Carson could have had a look round, could have had his tea, but he remembers thinking that this is the race she's been bred for, this is the race of her life, and he kept pushing with those tired arms all the way to the line.

Next time out she pulled too hard for her own good in the King George and had nothing left for the final furlong, but in the Yorkshire Oaks Carson determined to let 'er rip and she made all for a four-length victory. The St Leger was a triumph of her staying power and wily Carson's sleight of mouth – "I said that the ground was okay for her, but it was soft, so I kept her wide on better ground and even though she stretched my arms again we got away with it" – and provided a second Classic by three-quarters of a length from Esprit Du Nord.

If it hadn't been for All Along's astonishing luck in the Longchamp traffic Sun Princess would have added the Prix de l'Arc de Triomphe to her laurels, but after leading a long way from home she was just run out of it in a thrilling finish in which five of the first six were females, four of whom are included in this book.

Her four-year-old campaign was a disappointment, but at stud her first foal was the unlucky Prince Of Dance, who was put down during his three-year-old season after suffering from spinal cancer. "He was possibly the best I ever rode – he was better than Nashwan at home," adds Carson, before returning to the filly who produced him. "She was very special," he says. Twelve lengths proves it.

STEVE DENNIS

> "Five furlongs from home my arms were so tired I couldn't hold on to her any longer. I didn't send her on, she just took me there"

**Foaled**
May 18, 1980
**Pedigree**
English Prince –
Sunny Valley
**Breeder**
Ballymacoll Stud
**Owner**
Sir Michael Sobell
**Trainer**
Dick Hern
**Main jockey**
Willie Carson
**Career record**
Three wins and five
places from ten runs
**Most famous for**
Her 12-length victory
in the Oaks is the
joint-longest in a British
Classic since 1900
**Stud record**
Dam of eight winners
including ill-fated
Dewhurst Stakes winner
(dead heat) Prince
Of Dance

READY TO RUMBLE: Sun Princess and Willie Carson go to post before winning the Oaks by 12 lengths – the joint-longest in a British Classic since 1900

# 26

## KINCSEM

It is right and proper that we admire horses who run up fabulous sequences – think Sea The Stars, the well-known grammatical error Big Buck's and of course Frankel, who rattled up 14 in a row and took us to places unexplored.

But they are mere layabouts compared with the fabulous Kincsem, who ran 54 times and won the lot of them back in the 1870s.

Nor were all her wins in her native Hungary. In 1878 she came to Britain and won the Goodwood Cup before hopping across the Channel to add the Grand Prix de Deauville to her triumphant haul.

She was foaled in 1874 at the Hungarian National Stud while her owner-breeder Ernest von Blascovich was still in his 20s. He tried to sell a job lot of seven foals to Baron Orczy who took just five, rejecting Kincsem and one other as "too common-looking". She was no beauty, being "long as a boat, U-necked, gangling, mule-eared and with a tail like a badly used mop".

So von Blascovich put her into training with the British-born Robert Hesp, who was huntsman to Prince Batthyany – who later bred St Simon. Hesp rose high as an agent in the Hungarian secret service before returning to training. He ran Kincsem ten times in ten different cities at two and the following season she won 17. In 42 of her races she was ridden, almost always from behind, by Manchester-born Elijah Madden.

She had a habit of grazing at the start and once established as a Hungarian national heroine – a status she still enjoys today – plenty of folklore sprang up around her.

She kicked off her four-year-old career on April 22, 1878 as the unbeaten winner of 27 races. She proceeded to win nine races over five weeks –

twice in Vienna over three days, once at Pozsony, three in Budapest in five days, then back to Vienna for three victories in four days at the end of May.

She then had a break as von Blascovich and Hesp had long fancied a tilt at the Goodwood Cup followed by a raid on Deauville. At Goodwood, with her main rival a late non-runner, the mare raised the roof when winning as the crowd knew the sheer amount of travelling Kincsem undertook was unprecedented.

Triumphant she went back over the Channel to France and, having disembarked from her ship, there came one of those occasions that give a window into the great mare's soul.

Kincsem was devoted to two living creatures and would go nowhere without them. One was her lad Frankie and the other was a cat named Csalogany, with whom she was obsessed.

Kincsem was standing on the quay waiting to load onto a train but suddenly the cat was nowhere to be found. For two hours Kincsem planted herself

> **"There were three days of official mourning in Hungary and her passing was reported worldwide"**

**Foaled**
March 17, 1874
**Pedigree**
Cambuscan –
Waternymph
**Breeder**
Ernest von Blascovich
**Owner**
Ernest von Blascovich
**Trainer**
Robert Hesp
**Main jockey**
Elijah Madden
**Career record**
54 wins from 54 runs
**Most famous for**
Being an undefeated
and intrepid international
traveller victorious in
three Grosser Preis von
Baden, the Goodwood
Cup and Grand Prix
de Deauville
**Fate at stud**
Died aged 13 but
nonetheless an influential
continental taproot mare

and would not move, hollering constantly for her feline friend. Eventually Csalogany came running back, leapt on the mare's back and she walked onto the train without a bother on her.

She won narrowly at Deauville and then dead-heated for the Grosser Preis von Baden before winning a run-off easily.

Kincsem worked hard for a living but she was well looked after by Hesp and von Blascovich. All grain and hay came from her owner's stud and they brought vast amounts of water from home when she was on tour as she would drink nothing else.

But once in Baden her water ran out and for three days she would not touch a drop – no mean achievement in that spa town. But the resourceful Frankie found an old well and she would drink the water from that. It is known as Kincsem's Well to this day.

They say that one bitter night Kincsem awoke and spotted Frankie curled up near her with no covering.

She pulled off her blanket and dropped it on him – never wearing one at night again and always doing the same if given one. Frankie had no known surname and did his military service as Frankie Kincsem, and his grave bore the same name.

She was an iron-tough mare who would travel anywhere as long as cat and lad were with her. She died from colic aged 13 on March 17 – the exact anniversary of her birth. Her trainer Hesp was dead 39 days later.

There were three days of official mourning in Hungary and her passing was reported worldwide.

She proved a highly influential broodmare although, as Messrs Mortimer, Onslow and Willett remark in their *Encyclopaedia of British Flat Racing*: "Unfortunately there were heavy casualties among her descendants in both world wars."

Now there is a line we do not ever need to read again.
ALASTAIR DOWN

**FINE SPECIMEN:**
**Kincsem had a remarkable racing record of 54 races and 54 wins in the 1870s**

# 27

## FOUND

Found has been some find. A Prix Marcel Boussac winner at two, a Breeders' Cup Turf winner at three and an Arc winner at four – she has given us so many magical moments.

Sluggish in spring but awesome in autumn, this delightful daughter of Galileo and Lockinge heroine Red Evie will be remembered most for beating the boys and leading home an Aidan O'Brien 1–2–3 in the 2016 Arc at Chantilly.

The telltale signs arrived early. You don't win Curragh maidens on your debut unless you are very good and you certainly don't win Curragh maidens over a mile from stall 15 unless you are very, very good. Found achieved the feat on the second-last Sunday in August, 2014, swooping late to conquer subsequent Fillies' Mile winner Together Forever, who

**SUPER TOUGH: Found lands the Prix de l'Arc de Triomphe under Ryan Moore at Chantilly in 2016**

**Foaled**
March 13, 2012
**Pedigree**
Galileo – Red Evie
**Breeders**
Roncon, Wynatt &
Chelston
**Owners**
Michael Tabor,
Derrick Smith
and Sue Magnier
**Trainer**
Aidan O'Brien
**Main jockey**
Ryan Moore
**Career record**
Six wins and 14 places
from 21 runs
**Most famous for**
Leading home an Aidan
O'Brien 1–2–3 in the Prix
de l'Arc de Triomphe at
Chantilly in October 2016

Oh ye of little faith. Having been agonisingly denied in the Irish 1,000 Guineas and again in the Coronation Stakes at Royal Ascot, Found continued her frustrating sequence of seconds in the Irish Champion Stakes behind Golden Horn and the British equivalent at Ascot when unable to reel in the mud-loving Fascinating Rock. So often the bridesmaid, never the bride.

But, when her big day finally arrived, boy did she hog the limelight. It was at Keeneland on the final day of October. The Breeders' Cup Turf. Bright lights. The eyes of the world watching. This was supposed to be the sweetest of swansongs for Golden Horn, but instead Found pounced late under a textbook Ryan Moore ride.

O'Brien, usually so nonchalant, so calm, could not hide his admiration this time. "Found is a very special mare," he beamed. "To run in two Champion Stakes, an Arc and then to come and win the Breeders' Cup Turf is quite remarkable."

However, it was not quite as remarkable as what she did in 2016. Second in the Tattersalls Gold Cup, second in the Coronation Cup, second in the Prince of Wales's Stakes, second in the Yorkshire Oaks and second in the Irish Champion Stakes. Would her persistence and consistency ever be rewarded.

It was, you know, and on the biggest day of all.

O'Brien had been preaching all season about Found's season revolving around an autumn campaign and he had her perfectly tuned for Chantilly on the first Sunday in October.

Settled beautifully on the inner by Moore, she edged to the front shortly after the two-furlong pole and never looked like being caught afterwards. She was far too good for the globetrotting superstar Highland Reel, with Order Of St George completing the tricast for the Ballydoyle team.

"We've had our eye on this for a long time with Found," said O'Brien at Chantilly. "When Ryan rode her as a two-year-old, he said she could win an Arc one day. How right he was."

Moore knew.

"She's been frustrating sometimes but this has probably been the main aim all year," said Moore. "She was back to a mile and a half in an evenly run race and she showed what she's capable of. At her best she's a very hard filly to beat."

Her consistency was remarkable – she was runner-up in ten Group 1 races. Her class unquestioned – she won three Group 1s. Will we ever find another Found? Doubtful.

DAVID JENNINGS

> **"When Ryan Moore rode her as a two-year-old, he said she could win an Arc one day. How right he was"**

hailed from the same stable and had an eyecatching Galway run behind Legatissimo under her belt.

"She wouldn't have been able to come from where she was off such a slow pace unless she was smart," admitted O'Brien at the time.

Smart indeed. So smart that she blew away the French filly Ervedya on only her third start in the 2014 Prix Marcel Boussac on Arc day to finish off her juvenile career in style. Had we found the 1,000 Guineas winner?

Afraid not. She failed to make Newmarket as O'Brien did not want to rush her. Instead she reappeared at three in the Group 3 Athasi Stakes where she was stuffed by 25-1 outsider Iveagh Gardens. Perhaps she had not trained on. Maybe we had seen the best of her at two.

STUNNING SETTING:
Found exercises at Santa
Anita in November 2016
before her attempt to follow
up victory in the previous
year's Breeders' Cup Turf.
The Arc heroine failed in
her bid when finishing
third behind stablemate
Highland Reel

# 28

## WINX

Wondermare Winx is the darling of the Australian racing scene, the successor to the massively popular Black Caviar in the hearts of the Aussie racing public. Unlike the iconic sprinter, this new superstar is not unbeaten – but in the summer of 2017 was in the midst of a 17-race winning streak featuring no fewer than nine Group 1s at distances ranging from six and a half furlongs to a mile and three, including back-to-back successes in the Cox Plate.

After an eight-length demolition of a high-class field in the nation's top weight-for-age contest, Winx became the highest-rated turf horse in the world according to international handicappers with an official rating of 132 – the same as Black Caviar's best. "She is a superior racehorse," says her jockey Hugh Bowman. "It is just a great honour to be a part of it."

Like the great US racemare Zenyatta, Winx is a daughter of the Dubai World Cup winner Street Cry; she was sold for A$230,000 at the 2013 Magic Millions Gold Coast sale and sent to leading Sydney-based trainer Chris Waller.

Although she won the first three races of her career, Winx did not start to look anything out of the ordinary until the end of her three-year-old campaign, when she began her sensational winning spree with her final two starts, landing her first Group 1 success at odds-on in the Queensland Oaks.

Despite a comfortable victory that day, it would have been difficult to forecast what was to come as Winx stormed through her four-year-old campaign. In a noteworthy weight-carrying effort, she overcame serious interference to win the historic Epsom Handicap over a mile at Randwick before blowing away an international field on her Melbourne debut in the Cox Plate in a performance right out of the top drawer.

Dropped in by Bowman, she breezed up the inside on the final bend and won easily by nearly five lengths over four-time Group 1 winner Criterion with renowned Irish globe-trotter Highland Reel further back in third. For good measure, she also broke the Moonee Valley track record.

After a three-and-a-half-month break, Winx carried on where she left off as she returned to Sydney for the autumn and rattled off four more wins, rounding off her campaign by defying top weight on soft ground against 14 rivals in the Doncaster Handicap. On the ratings, this was the best performance of her career to date (RPR 127) – and it hadn't come easily as she faced a wall of horses inside the final furlong before breaking through for a two-length victory.

The only surprise about Winx being voted Australian Horse of the Year at the end of the season was that she did not receive every available vote. One person voted against, and they probably felt foolish given the mare's exploits in the first half of her five-year-old campaign as she went from strength to strength with three Group victories before her Cox Plate tour de force in October.

The race looked to be on as she ranged alongside her main rival, the Melbourne Cup favourite Hartnell, but if this was a race, it was of the one-horse variety. The response when Bowman popped the question was electric: Winx took a two-length lead at the head of the straight and drew further and further away to score by a record winning margin that left the crowd going mad and her trainer fighting back the tears.

"She was just in the zone and wherever she goes, if she's in that zone, she'll win anything," says Waller. "She is just such an athlete. She has a tremendous will to win. She comes from impossible positions in races, overcomes wide draws or wet tracks, the kind of things most horses at the highest grade struggle with."

Although Waller mentioned Royal Ascot as a possibility for 2017, he later outlined a programme at home revolving around a bid to become only the second horse ever to win three Cox Plates. Whatever else she achieves, however, Winx has already done enough to earn her place among the immortals.

"I never thought when she was a young horse this was where she would get to," says Waller. "She is something special."

NICHOLAS GODFREY

"She was just in the zone and if she's in the zone, she'll win anything"

ARMS HELD ALOFT:
Hugh Bowman and Winx return after completing back-to-back victories in the Cox Plate at Randwick in October 2016

**Foaled**
September 14, 2011
**Pedigree**
Street Cry –
Vegas Showgirl
**Breeder**
Fairway Thoroughbreds
**Owners**
Magic Bloodstock Racing, Richard Treweeke and Debbie Kepitis
**Trainer**
Chris Waller
**Main jockey**
Hugh Bowman
**Career record**
21 wins and three places from 27 runs
**Most famous for**
Australian superstar's winning streak now stretches to 17 races, most recent among them an eight-length Cox Plate annihilation in October 2016, after which she was rated the world's number one turf performer

# 29
## STANERRA

Lord, she was tough. Stanerra was not so much foaled as hewn from the rock on which Moyglare Stud stands and anything less like a traditional fairytale heroine would be hard to imagine – yet fairytale it was.

The first chapters of Stanerra's life do not detain us long, which is just as well given the extent of what followed. Unraced at two, twice raced at three when with Jim Bolger, Stanerra's formative years offered no hint of the hard case she would become. Two runs in two seasons? In her ferocious prime she would manage that workload within a week.

Her life changed when she was bought by department store tycoon Frank Dunne, who masterminded her monumental ascent as trainer as well as owner. This was unconventional, sure, but no more than the rest of the narrative.

In some way Dunne diagnosed the bottomless reserves of resolve in his mare and set about liberating them. By the end of the 1982 season she had run 13 times, graduated into Group company – third in the Hardwicke, second in the Sun Chariot – and undertaken an unlikely assault on the Japan Cup, in which she finished fourth. Yet it was all merely an hors d'oeuvre for a truly remarkable five-year-old campaign in 1983. Like the proof of Fermat's Last Theorem, this space is almost too small to contain it.

> "On the Friday she was practically running away with me. Oh, she was amazing, had a tremendous constitution"

In June, with her first Group-race success behind her and a new alliance forged with jockey Brian Rouse, the tall, rangy Stanerra held an entry in two races at Royal Ascot, the (then Group 2) Prince of Wales's Stakes on the Tuesday and the Hardwicke Stakes on the Friday. Many horses have a similar agenda and they run in one or the other. Not Stanerra; that would be not enough like hard work. She ran in both and won both.

The Prince of Wales's Stakes was almost a warm-up – she sneaked through on the rail and powered clear to win by four lengths, bouncing off the firm ground like a rubber ball. It was easy, but not as easy as it was three days later, when Rouse could hardly hold her as she barrelled into the lead off the home turn. Only Electric could make a race of it, going down by a length and a half with the Group 1-winning Be My Native 12 lengths adrift in third. And, just to show incontrovertibly what manner of mare she was, to show that her earlier exertions were not weighing heavy on her legs, Stanerra broke the course record set eight years earlier in that unparalleled Grundy-Bustino race for the King George.

"She was a big, strong mare, a bit of a character," says Rouse. "Nothing nasty, but she had her own ideas about how to do things sometimes.

"I was delighted with her at Ascot on the Tuesday, told Frank that she hadn't had a particularly hard race, so he said she could go again. On the Friday she was practically running away with me. Oh, she was amazing, had a tremendous constitution."

Stanerra was then beaten about a length into fourth in a bunch finish for the Eclipse, strolled home in front of an adoring home crowd in the Joe McGrath Memorial Stakes and came off worst of six in another hectic finish, this time for the Prix de l'Arc de Triomphe. Dunne brought her home, looked her in the eye, saw that the fire was still alight. Next stop Japan.

"When she got off the plane she was all tied-up, she was pretty bad," remembers Rouse. "She couldn't be ridden, all we could do was lead her around for a few hours a day. She had one canter on the Friday and that was all the work she did before the race."

It was enough. Given a shrewd inside-outside local's ride by Rouse, Stanerra immersed herself in yet another titanic battle down the stretch before grinding out victory by a head, becoming the first European winner of the Japan Cup. "I couldn't believe it," says Rouse. Yes, Stanerra was like that.

STEVE DENNIS

**Foaled**
May 4, 1978
**Pedigree**
Guillaume Tell – Lady Aureola
**Breeder**
Moyglare Stud
**Owner**
Frank Dunne
**Trainers**
Jim Bolger and Frank Dunne
**Main jockey**
Brian Rouse
**Career record**
Seven wins and five places from 24 runs
**Most famous for**
The iron constitution that enabled her to conquer the world as a five-year-old
**Fate at stud**
One winner of a minor race from six known foals

DOUBLE DELIGHT:
Stanerra and Brian Rouse are led in after winning the Hardwicke Stakes at Royal Ascot in 1983 – three days after landing the Prince of Wales's Stakes

# 30
## BALANCHINE

Sheikh Mohammed is fond of saying that the race for excellence has no finish line. That may be so, but it surely has a start line and Balanchine was the horse standing astride it. She may not have been Godolphin's Case Zero (that was Cutwater, or Day-flower), but she was their first big-race winner – after her, the deluge.

Unbeaten in two minor races at two, Balanchine had demonstrated considerable promise and it was something of a surprise when owner-breeder Robert Sangster sold her to his old sale-ring nemesis Sheikh Mohammed, whose Godolphin project was still at the experimental stage. As a result, the filly spent the winter in Dubai with one-season trainer Hilal Ibrahim instead of in Britain, the idea being that she would return for the Classics with a clear developmental advantage over her stay-at-home peers.

The outcome of the 1,000 Guineas indicated that Sheikh Mohammed might be on to something. Balanchine – a 20-1 shot running in Maktoum Al Maktoum's blue and white silks, the 'Godolphin' horses running for their individual owners at that stage – arrived in Britain four days before the race and was beaten only a short head by Las Meninas (owned, in a neat twist, by Sangster). The race commentary noted her as 'running for Dubai' – the world was changing.

That stout-hearted display ushered Balanchine towards the Oaks, where Frankie Dettori would wear the red cap of the second-string before playing the

---

**"I knew at the furlong pole it would take a machine to pass us, we were going so fast"**

**Foaled**
April 16, 1991
**Pedigree**
Storm Bird –
Morning Devotion
**Breeder**
Swettenham Stud
**Owners**
Robert Sangster and
Godolphin
**Trainers**
Peter Chapple-Hyam,
Hilal Ibrahim and
Saeed Bin Suroor
**Main jockey**
Frankie Dettori
**Career record**
Four wins and two places
from eight runs
**Most famous for**
Being Godolphin's first
Classic winner and
beating the colts in the
Irish Derby
**Fate at stud**
Four minor winners from
seven foals to race

**OFF THE MARK:** a joyous
Frankie Dettori after
claiming a first Classic
success in Britain on
Balanchine in the 1994
Oaks at Epsom

starring role. In windy, wet conditions far removed from all that Dubai sunshine, the white-faced Balanchine went to her task with a will, racing prominently before staying on grittily up the hill to win going away by two and a half lengths. It was Dettori's first British Classic win and commentator Graham Goode did not miss the wider significance, saying: "What a triumph this is for the Emirates team."

The Emirates team were busy turning racing's received wisdom on its head and were not about to pause for reflection. Balanchine was aimed at the Irish Derby (fellow Oaks winner Salsabil had trod the same path with success four years earlier) where she would take on Sheikh Mohammed's Derby runner-up King's Theatre. This was the exciting essence of the fledgling Godolphin project in which convention was openly defied and the brilliant Balanchine was the ideal vehicle with which to make an enduring impact.

She was still only third-favourite at the Curragh but she outran any lingering doubts and all her rivals with an exhilarating elan, leading into the straight and galloping on relentlessly to see off King's Theatre by four and a half lengths. "I knew at the furlong pole it would take a machine to pass us, we were going so fast," said Dettori. "No words can describe her, she was unbelievable, much better than at Epsom."

It was Balanchine's finest hour, her position in the annals secure, both by beating the boys in a Classic and by proving that the Dubai experiment could work. It was, unfortunately, almost Balanchine's final hour, as a couple of weeks later she went down with serious colic and survived only after an emergency operation. It meant the end of her campaign, although not her career. When she returned to action the following summer, however, her considerable sparkle was absent.

Now under the care of Saeed Bin Suroor, she was soundly defeated at Royal Ascot before hinting at recovery when beaten a short head by Carnegie in an Arc trial, but a lacklustre display in the Arc itself was Balanchine's last dance. It is likely the effects of the colic and the operation denied her the chance of greater glories, but it would be ridiculous to view Balanchine's exploits in the light of what might have been, for what she did during her brief career left a legacy both on the racecourse and off it.

When purchasing Balanchine, Sheikh Mohammed might reasonably have thought he was buying a horse who would one day become a foundation mare. That did not come to pass – instead he had bought himself a horse who would be a foundation.
STEVE DENNIS

# 31
## DUNFERMLINE

Timing is everything. The good fortune of her foaling date meant that Dunfermline was a three-year-old in 1977, which happened to be quite a special year for her owner and, by extension, the whole of Britain. One year either way and she was simply a very talented filly who won two Classics – instead, she was in the right place at the right time to lend a golden glow to the Silver Jubilee celebrations.

Circumstance was not the only factor in her favour. She was a strong stayer in a year when that virtue was relatively thinly spread, and she was trained by a man whose unhurried style allowed her to peak when it mattered most. There was nothing overly precocious about Dunfermline, who ended her juvenile campaign as a three-race maiden, al-

**JUBILEE JOY:** Dunfermline and Willie Carson complete a Classic double in the St Leger at Doncaster when getting the better of Alleged and Lester Piggott in what was a special year for the filly's owner, Her Majesty The Queen

**Foaled**
April 15, 1974
**Pedigree**
Royal Palace –
Strathcona
**Breeder**
The Queen
**Owner**
The Queen
**Trainer**
Dick Hern
**Main jockey**
Willie Carson
**Career record**
Three wins and six places
from 12 runs
**Most famous for**
Winning two Classics
in her owner-breeder's
Silver Jubilee year
**Fate at stud**
No winners from
four foals

failed to stay, but Dunfermline relished the test and the fast pace set by Vaguely Deb. She was under strong driving even on the descent to Tattenham Corner, Willie Carson pushing energetically away in his trademark style, but she made relentless headway in the straight, drew level with the Luca Cumani-trained Freeze The Secret in the final furlong, and her resolution and stamina saw her home by three-quarters of a length.

Her success was hugely popular with the public, coming as it did in the central week of the Silver Jubilee festivities. Carson calls it the highlight of his long and glittering career. "That race is stamped in my heart," he says, although his willing partner is not quite so high in his affections.

"She didn't have much personality and wasn't a spectacular type," says Carson. "She had no turn of foot, you had to really wind her up, but once she was rolling along she kept on going.

"She was like a colt, really, just got on with the job, didn't lie down when things got tough. And she stayed very, very well."

Next time out Dunfermline was third in a slowly run Yorkshire Oaks – "I didn't use her stamina sensibly," says Carson – but the St Leger was expected to play to her strengths, and she would have the help of a pacemaker in Gregarious. It looked as though she would need all the help she could get, though, with the odds-on and unbeaten favourite Alleged in opposition.

His rider Lester Piggott may have believed Alleged was unbeatable, even at this extended trip, and went for home with half a mile still to run. It was a tactical blunder as it gave Dunfermline something to chase, her ideal scenario, and when Carson got her rolling she cut into Alleged's lead, joined him, passed him a furlong out, and stuck dourly to the task to prevail by a length and a half. They had drawn clear in compelling fashion; the third horse was ten lengths adrift.

"It was a full-on duel for the last two furlongs and she just wouldn't give in," recalls Carson. Dunfermline thus became the only horse ever to beat dual Arc winner Alleged.

Indeed, three weeks later Alleged had Dunfermline back in fourth at Longchamp and the rest of the filly's career was a disappointment. She might have excelled as a Cup horse the following year, but was never given that opportunity. Her place in history was secure, though. Cometh the hour, cometh the horse – of all the Queen's horses, Dunfermline timed it best.
STEVE DENNIS

beit one with two places in Group company to her credit. Moreover, in three races at four she showed little of her previous sparkle. Truly, Dunfermline timed it right.

Her placed efforts in the May Hill Stakes and the Fillies' Mile suggested middle distances would show her off to best effect and her first outing at three – a four-length defeat of subsequent Irish Oaks winner Olwyn (although the Irish Oaks was a poor race that year) in the Pretty Polly Stakes at Newmarket – indicated her Classic pretensions and the mile and a half of the Oaks looked certain to suit.

It did and, more to the point, it didn't suit her market rivals. All those above her in the betting

> "She was like a colt, really, just got on with the job, didn't lie down when things got tough. And she stayed very well"

# 32
## PARK TOP

It might be assumed that a champion mare carrying the distinctive pale silks of the Cavendish family might have been the result of either a stellar mating arranged by her owner-breeder, the 11th Duke of Devonshire, or else a high-stakes purchase at the sales.

Park Top was neither, having cost trainer Bernard van Cutsem just 500 guineas as a yearling at Tattersalls in 1965.

She was slow to recoup even that modest outlay, failing to reach the track at two. But she was already showing plenty at home before bolting up on her debut at Windsor, the prelude to her defeat of the Oaks runner-up at Royal Ascot.

Mick Ryan, van Cutsem's assistant and a future Classic-winning trainer in his own right, takes up the story.

"We knew before she went to Windsor that she was very professional at home and it hadn't gone unnoticed among the lads, so we all had a good few quid on her," Ryan says. "When she met St Pauli Girl in the Ribblesdale, poor old Humphrey Cottrill thought his was a certainty and I had to say to him, 'Don't be surprised if this one comes and gets you'. Fillies who were unlucky in the Oaks always seemed to get turned over in the Ribblesdale."

Although Park Top became a dual winner of the Brighton Cup as well as picking up a decent prize at Longchamp the following year, it would be the summer of 1969 before she fully realised her potential, when a hat-trick of impressive victories earned her widespread popularity.

"She had an absolutely enormous turn of foot, but unfortunately she had to be held up for a late burst," says Ryan. "Sometimes it happened for her and – just ask Geoff Lewis – sometimes it didn't. In

that respect she was her own worst enemy in a race if it didn't go right. [Lester] Piggott was a master on her and if you could get her covered up behind a fast pace on good ground, she could go from 0 to 60 in ten seconds and pass good horses like they were standing still."

That certainly summed up Piggott's tactics when Park Top slipstreamed Connaught and Mount Athos before pouncing late to land the Coronation Cup at Epsom.

An easy success in the Hardwicke followed, before Park Top and the deputising Lewis found all kinds of trouble in a slowly run Eclipse at Sandown.

But Park Top's winning streak would soon be restored with Piggott back in the saddle when she surged from last to first to see off Crozier and Hogarth in the King George VI and Queen Elizabeth Stakes.

"When she won the King George, I will never for-

HALLOWED TURF: Park Top and Lester Piggott return to the winner's enclosure after landing the 1969 King George VI and Queen Elizabeth Stakes at Ascot

**Foaled**
May 1964
**Pedigree**
Kalydon – Nellie Park
**Breeder**
Buttermilk Stud Farm
**Owner**
11th Duke of Devonshire
**Trainer**
Bernard van Cutsem
**Main jockey**
Lester Piggott
**Career record**
13 wins and eight places
from 24 runs
**Most famous for**
Winning the Coronation
Cup, Hardwicke Stakes
and King George VI and
Queen Elizabeth Stakes
as a five-year-old during
a golden seven-week
spell in the summer of
1969
**Fate at stud**
Produced three
winners – none of her
quality – but is granddam
and great-granddam of
Group winners in both
North and South America

get the ovation she got coming into the winner's enclosure," says Ryan. "As for the Eclipse, Geoff [Lewis] came in and told me she just didn't seem to be moving right coming round the bend. I said: 'Geoff, if I were you I'd get that saddle off as quick as you can and make a beeline for the weighing room. I don't think that's quite gonna get away with it.'"

Park Top then went to Longchamp, winning her Arc prep in the Prix Foy, only to be the victim of traffic problems on the big day when second to the Ascot Gold Cup winner, Levmoss, who had beaten her a year earlier at Newbury. Levmoss was the beneficiary of a fine ride from Bill Williamson, while Piggott blamed himself for Park Top's defeat.

Ryan says: "Piggott rode a lot for us in those days at van Cutsem's but I'd never seen him like that before. He was really upset about that one. She should have won the Arc."

Park Top raced on at six but, in an injury interrupted campaign, could add only La Coupe at Longchamp and the Cumberland Lodge Stakes at Ascot to her roll of honour, while her swansong in the Prix Royallieu ended with an ignominious reception from the Longchamp turfistes.

"What nobody realised was that she had been struck into," says Ryan. "The Parisians don't take it lightly when a short one gets beat and they were all booing. The Duke of Devonshire turned round and gave the old two-fingered salute and the place went berserk.

"We had plenty of good fillies but if everything went right she had a phenomenal turn of foot and, in all the years I was in racing, I never came across a horse who could put a race to sleep in such a short time."
SCOTT BURTON

> "When she won the King George I will never forget the ovation she got coming into the winner's enclosure"

# 33

## SNOW FAIRY

It may seem strange to say it of a filly whose three-year-old career yielded Classics in both England and Ireland, but it is for faraway successes in the early hours of the morning that Snow Fairy deserves to be remembered.

Having been bought back by her owner Cristina Patino for just €1,800 as an unwanted lot at the yearling sales, she managed just a Lingfield maiden auction success from six starts as a two-year-old and did not even warrant an entry in the Oaks.

So it is beyond dispute that the daughter of Intikhab proved something of a surprise package when winning the Height Of Fashion Stakes at Goodwood as the opening volley of her three-year-old season, and even more so when she won the Epsom showpiece itself on her next start under a daredevil ride from Ryan Moore and then enjoyed an eight-length romp in the Curragh equivalent.

But it wasn't until she headed for the Far East in November 2010 that the full extent of her majesty was unveiled. Shrugging off a fall while in quarantine that left her with badly scraped knees, she made off with first the Queen Elizabeth II Commemorative Cup at Kyoto, then the Hong Kong Cup at Sha Tin, to bolster the reputations of both Moore and globetrotting trainer Ed Dunlop, but mostly to estab-lish beyond all doubt her own star quality and true grit.

The following year Snow Fairy fell agonisingly short in a series of Group 1s in Europe but once again shone in the face of adversity when asked to add to her gains in Asia. Bitten by an unidentified bug while in quarantine in Tokyo, she was long odds even to line up in her second QEII, but the renowned Dunlop travelling team and the Japanese vets worked their magic.

"Her whole body and legs had swollen up, she was lame and her blood picture went through the floor," recalls Dunlop. "She was then treated with some form of fly spray which had a major reaction and took the skin off the inside of her hind legs, to go with the large haematoma between her front legs.

"It looked highly unlikely she was going to run, and it was touch and go right up to the day, but we got her there and in the end Ryan produced a masterful ride on an amazing filly. She was the first international horse to land this race and I think people are now beginning to realise how hard it is to win in Japan."

For Moore, victory on Snow Fairy in the Prix Jean Romanet at Deauville the following August (later disqualified after testing positive for a banned substance) completed a perfect six Group 1s from six rides on Snow Fairy, but Dunlop maintains that her best was left until last, under another rider, in the Irish Champion Stakes, in which she got the better of a mighty tussle with Nathaniel and St Nicholas Abbey.

In the tender hands of Frankie Dettori, she was held up off a ferocious pace, travelling in her comfort zone until asked to make ground smoothly, arriving on the scene going best of all and hitting the front at the furlong pole.

Any worries that the tendon injury that had kept her off the course for ten months prior to Deauville might inhibit her finishing effort were quickly dispelled as she battled tenaciously to fend off two top-drawer challengers.

Sadly, injury ended her career soon afterwards, but the patience of owner and trainer, allied to her own supreme toughness and resilience, gave her that chance of a memorable swansong.

"Most owners would have retired her a lot sooner than Mrs Patino did," says a grateful Dunlop, "and if this had been the case she would not have won the Irish Champion Stakes, which was without doubt her greatest performance."

The greatest in a very strong line-up of Group 1 races across four countries, it has to be said.

PETER THOMAS

> **"In the tender hands of Frankie Dettori, she was held up off a ferocious pace, travelling in her comfort zone until asked to make ground smoothly"**

**Foaled**
February 12, 2007
**Pedigree**
Intikhab –
Woodland Dream
**Breeder**
Windflower Overseas
Holdings Inc
**Owner**
Anamoine Limited
**Trainer**
Ed Dunlop
**Main jockeys**
Ryan Moore
and Frankie Dettori
**Career record**
Eight wins and eight
places from 21 runs
**Most famous for**
Six wins at the top level,
including two Classics,
an Irish Champion Stakes
and three globetrotting
successes in Japan and
Hong Kong
**Fate at stud**
Her 2015 filly foal
Belle De Neige, by
Elusive Pimpernel, is
eagerly awaited, as
are the products of her
matings with Palavicini
and Gleneagles

FAN CLUB: Snow Fairy with her jubilant connections after the 2012 Irish Champion Stakes at Leopardstown in what proved to be her final start in an illustrious career

ONE HORSE TOWN:
Snow Fairy leaves her rivals
trailing in her wake in the
Irish Oaks at the Curragh
in 2010

POOL ANTICS: Snow
Fairy goes for a swim at
Ed Dunlop's La Grange
Stables in Newmarket
in the summer of 2013

LOOK OF JOY: Frankie
Dettori shows his delight
after Snow Fairy defeats
Nathaniel in the 2012 Irish
Champion Stakes

# 34

# MAKYBE DIVA

Although Makybe Diva had plenty of form in top-class weight-for-age company, it is thanks to her amazing record in the Melbourne Cup that she has every right to be labelled a legend.

Only five horses have triumphed more than once in the fabled contest which is reputed to stop a nation. Only one has won three times, however, and that was Makybe Diva, who earned a deserved place in the pantheon – and the affections of the Australian public – with her hat-trick in the years between 2003 to 2005. She won seven Group 1s altogether, including a Cox Plate.

"She transcends the sport," suggested trainer Lee Freedman when she was retired. Few would have argued.

An Australian icon bred in Britain, Makybe Diva was owned by tuna-fishing millionaire Tony Santic, who named her using the first two letters from the names of five of his female employees. The filly was shipped to Australia and put into training with David Hall, for whom she was to progress through the ranks with a six-race winning spree as a three-year-old in Melbourne.

Her first visit to the race she was to make her own came at the age of four in November 2003 when she was partnered by Glen Boss, who was to become synonymous with her over the years to come.

Known as 'Group 1 Glen' owing to his record in the top races, the Sydney-based rider fitted Makybe Diva like a glove. After holding up his filly, Boss picked his way through the Cup field to take the Flemington two-miler by a length and a half. She went on to become the first mare ever to complete the Melbourne Cup/Sydney Cup double by winning the latter at Randwick in the Australian autumn.

**Foaled**
March 21, 1999
**Pedigree**
Desert King – Tugela
**Breeder**
Emily Kristina (Aust) Pty Ltd
**Owner**
Emily Kristina Pty Ltd Syndicate (Tony Santic)
**Trainers**
Lee Freedman and David Hall
**Main jockey**
Glen Boss
**Career record**
15 wins and seven places from 36 runs
**Most famous for**
Australian racing great became Melbourne Cup legend with unprecedented hat-trick in 2003 to 2005
**Fate at stud**
Makybe Diva is a broodmare at her owner's property in Victoria, named Makybe after the superstar mare. Although foals offered at public auction have reached six-figure sums, none of her offspring have yet come close to matching her talent

"Everyone still talks about her. You ask them to name two or three winners of the Cup and they couldn't do it. But they all know Makybe Diva"

VICTORY SALUTE: Glen Boss waves to the crowd after riding Makybe Diva to her first of three Melbourne Cup successes in 2003

After Hall left for Hong Kong, the last two years of Makybe Diva's career were guided by leading trainer Lee Freedman. She came back better than ever at the next spring carnival, where she was duly sent off favourite to complete back-to-back Cup successes. She did so in grand style, hitting the front just over a furlong out and running on strongly to beat multiple Irish St Leger winner Vinnie Roe. Cue scenes of adulation from an adoring Flemington crowd.

While that second Cup ensured Makybe Diva became public property, she also possessed versatility and class in abundance, as she went on to demonstrate in the Australian autumn, breaking the track record for 2,000 metres (about 1m2f) in the Australian Cup at Flemington before a startling last-to-first burst to claim the BMW, Sydney's number one weight-for-age race at Rosehill.

Back in Melbourne the following spring, she was only a short head away from going undefeated in five Group races at distances ranging from seven furlongs to two miles; among them was the Cox Plate, in which she rounded a wall of horses for a decisive victory in the continent's premier weight-for-age contest.

In reality, though, her final campaign was all about one race, and the six-year-old Makybe Diva lined up for her third and final Cup with the weight of expectation, adulation and veneration on her shoulders. She let no-one down.

To the utter delight of a fervent crowd she took command a furlong and a half out to secure a comfortable length-and-a-half victory and a lasting place in racing folklore.

Choosing his words carefully, Freedman captured the mood. "Go find the smallest child on this course and there will be the only example of a person who will live long enough to see that again," said the trainer.

Having earned more than A$14.5 million (about £5.75m), Makybe Diva was retired as the highest-earning racehorse in Australian history; her legendary status soon given an official stamp when she retained her crown as Australian horse of the year, becoming only the third horse to claim the title more than once. She was inducted into the Hall of Fame in 2006, the same year that a life-sized bronze statue was erected at Flemington.

"Everyone still wants to talk about her," says Boss. "You ask them to name two or three other winners of the Cup and they couldn't do it. But they all know Makybe Diva."
NICHOLAS GODFREY

# 35

# HABIBTI

Anybody under the age of 35 can be forgiven for thinking that Lady Aurelia's seven-length win in the Queen Mary at Royal Ascot in June 2016 was the most breathtaking sprint performance by a filly that had ever been seen.

However, those racegoers of an older vintage will recall their emotions when Habibti won the Sprint Cup at Haydock by the same jaw-dropping margin during her triumphant summer in 1983.

Habibti's rider Willie Carson says: "I didn't ride too many top-class sprinters but along with Dayjur, who was the fastest I rode, she was one of the two who stand out – her record tells you she was quite special.

"I think the reason Dandy [David Nicholls, rider of Habibti's rival Soba] doesn't like me is I used to get upsides him on the bridle, turn to him, tell him to push harder and then off I'd go!"

The Spice Girls were still a decade away but girl power had engulfed sprinting, with Habibti's exploits coming hot on the heels of Marwell as the colts played second fiddle.

Habibti burst onto the scene at Ascot as her trainer John Dunlop remembers.

He says: "There was one funny thing about her debut over six furlongs considering she ended up doing most of her winning on straight courses – it was run around a bend because of problems with the straight course."

Had it not been for testing her stamina in the quest for Classic glory in early 1983 Habibti might have built a huge unbeaten run as she was undefeated in three races as a juvenile, winning her maiden before landing the Lowther, in which she beat subsequent Breeders' Cup Mile winner Royal Heroine.

**Foaled**
March 29, 1980
**Pedigree**
Habitat – Klairessa
**Breeder**
John Costelloe
**Owner**
Mohammed Mutawa
**Trainer**
John Dunlop
**Main jockey**
Willie Carson
**Career record**
Nine wins and six places from 17 runs
**Most famous for**
Winning the Sprint Cup by seven lengths
**Fate at stud**
Could not produce anything to match her own exploits. Essentially a flop with just two minor winners

# "I've got a picture of her winning over my desk in my study and there is not another horse in sight"

LAST HURRAH: Habibti records the final success of her career in the 1984 King's Stand Stakes at Royal Ascot

Not entered in the Cheveley Park, Habibti ended the season with success in the Group 1 Moyglare Stud Stakes.

After a fair fourth in the 1,000 Guineas at Newmarket, soft ground hindered her chance in the Irish equivalent and signalled a return to sprinting.

With Royal Ascot coming too soon Habibti started her dazzling run of wins in the July Cup and Dunlop says: "She annihilated them."

Carson did not need to reach for his whip and the five-time champion jockey, who rode more than 3,800 winners, has a daily reminder of that success.

He says: "I've got a picture of her winning over my desk in my study and there is not another horse in sight."

Carson adds: "The Vernons [Haydock Sprint Cup] was around a bend then and I remember John telling me you have plenty of time when you come around it.

"We came up the far side in the straight so it must have been on softer ground. I think I got there late but not as late as I did in the King's Stand a year later."

Habibti's three-year-old career ended with victory over 5f in the Abbaye and she was named Britain's Horse of the Year.

The 1984 King's Stand saw her make up six lengths on Irish challenger Anita's Prince in the last two furlongs and proved to be Habibti's last success.

Dunlop says: "She was a lovely character and a good-looking filly. She was a pleasure to deal with and quite remarkable."
BRUCE JACKSON

# 36
## SALSABIL

How do you follow the exploits of Nashwan? That was the question facing owner Hamdan Al Maktoum as 1990 dawned with the previous year's Guineas and Derby winner newly retired.

An 800,000 guineas investment in a filly by new stallion Sadler's Wells proved the answer as Salsabil matched Nashwan in winning her two British Classic assignments.

But she went one Classic better in her short career when landing the Irish Derby, which had not

IN FRONT: Salsabil and Willie Carson battle past Heart Of Joy to land the 1,000 Guineas at Newmarket in 1990

**Foaled**
January 18, 1987
**Pedigree**
Sadler's Wells –
Flame Of Tara
**Breeder**
Kilcarn Stud
**Owner**
Hamdan Al Maktoum
**Trainer**
John Dunlop
**Jockey**
Willie Carson
**Career record**
Seven wins and one
place from nine runs
**Most famous for**
Being the first filly since
1900 to beat the colts in
the 1990 Irish Derby
**Fate at stud**
Sadly succumbed to
colon cancer after just
five seasons at her
owner's Shadwell Stud.
Still produced Group
winners in Bint Salsabil,
who won four of her 11
races including the Group
3 Rockfel, and Alabaq,
successful in an Italian
Group 3

After narrowly losing out at Newbury next time Salsabil was boldly aimed at the Group 1 Prix Marcel Boussac on Arc weekend.

She repaid the confidence of Sheikh Hamdan by convincingly beating Houseproud, who was to go on to win the French 1,000 Guineas.

Salsabil's Classic season got off to the best possible start when she won the Fred Darling at Newbury by six lengths, with favourite Dead Certain – winner of the Queen Mary, Lowther and Cheveley Park – finishing distressed and tailed off in last.

Most of Salsabil's rivals were in distress some way out in the 1,000 Guineas, but she had to work hard to get past Nell Gwyn winner Heart Of Joy. The rest were five lengths and more back.

Carson remembers he had doubts about Salsabil's stamina before the Oaks as she showed so much speed, but her trainer John Dunlop was quoted as saying "she has a top-class middle-distance pedigree".

However, there was no reason for Carson to have lost any sleep as Salsabil galloped her rivals into the ground to win at Epsom by five lengths. But the best was still to come at the Curragh just 22 days later.

"The highlight of her career was winning the Irish Derby," says Dunlop. "She was an outstanding filly, a lovely, quality filly."

She faced not only the Derby one-two Quest For Fame and Blue Stag in Ireland but also Belmez, who was to go on to beat the previous year's Irish Derby winner Old Vic in the King George at Ascot.

Carson says: "It was an amazing weekend – I had ridden 22 winners in the week, had three rides in Ireland and they all won.

"The Irish Derby was one of the easiest races she ever had. A furlong and a half to run she was still on the bridle and went clear – race over."

Victory – albeit narrowly – in the Prix Vermeille sent her to the Arc a red-hot favourite, but there was no valedictory farewell.

Dunlop says: "She had a blood picture that was slightly off but not bad enough to pull her out and she was definitely below par that day."

Carson adds: "I won two Group 1s on the day but walked off the course with my head between my knees I was so disappointed. She was not herself and coughed after."

Salsabil remains the best filly sired by Sadler's Wells on Racing Post Ratings. What more needs saying?
BRUCE JACKSON

"A furlong and a half to run she was still on the bridle and went clear – race over"

been won by a filly since Gallinaria in 1900.

Less than nine months earlier the wraps were taken off Salsabil. Willie Carson, who rode her in all nine starts, recalls the impression she left on him after their debut romp in a 6f Nottingham maiden in September 1989 on firm ground.

He says: "I remember vividly saying you have a filly who is going to the top. I didn't realise how far she was going then but knew she was a bit special. She ended up being very special."

# 37

# TIME CHARTER

Anyone bewitched by the sterling deeds of Found would have been similarly enchanted by a mare who also had a lengthy and fulfilling career. Found won three Group or Grade 1 races from 21 starts; Time Charter won four from 20, together with the 1982 Sun Chariot Stakes, which was then a Group 2.

Then, as now, familiarity bred contentment. Time Charter raced for four seasons at a time when the programme for older fillies and mares was nothing like as obliging. They had little choice but to confront older colts, which made life tough for them.

Time Charter won the Oaks and Champion Stakes at three, the King George VI and Queen Elizabeth Stakes at four and the Coronation Cup at five, when she just failed to overhaul Sadler's Wells in the Eclipse. That neck defeat remains a huge lament in an otherwise fabulous career.

"I do think she should have won the Eclipse," says Henry Candy, who trained Time Charter and legged Joe Mercer into the saddle. "She was flying at the finish but I don't blame anybody. It was a big field and Sandown is a very tricky track to ride a waiting race. It also took her a while to get going."

The previous season Mercer had ridden Time Charter to win the 1983 King George, when her trademark late flourish saw her reel in the enterprisingly-ridden Diamond Shoal. She was only the second filly to win the race.

Time Charter put up two further outstanding performances over a mile and a half. She won the 1982 Oaks, in the process setting a record time for the fillies' classic. And she won the 1984 Coronation Cup under Steve Cauthen, who sat motionless as Time Charter cruised up to the previous year's 12-length Oaks heroine Sun Princess, before dismissing her by four contemptuous lengths.

"I would think that extraordinary victory in the Champion Stakes was probably the best of her career"

ROUSING FINISH: Time Charter (yellow cap) reels in the enterprisingly ridden Diamond Shoal in the 1983 King George VI and Queen Elizabeth Stakes at Ascot

Either victory might have made a career highlight, but Candy settles on the 1982 Champion Stakes, for which the Eclipse and King George winner, Kalaglow, started a warm favourite in the 14-strong field.

Time Charter was penned in along the stands' rail with more than two furlongs left to run. Undaunted, the three-year-old filly burst through a narrow gap between Kalaglow and Montekin, a pair of older males, before drawing right away to win by seven lengths. It was the longest winning distance in the illustrious history of the race.

"I would think that extraordinary victory was probably the best of her career," Candy says. "It was a fantastic effort, especially for a filly who was on the small side. Nothing could stay with her that day."

Victory in the Champion Stakes persuaded connections to abandon plans to retire Time Charter at the season's end and breed her to Northern Dancer. The feeling was that she'd had a long, hard campaign, which started in April when she won the Listed Masaka Stakes at Kempton by five lengths. After that she ran second in the 1,000 Guineas behind On The House before her record-breaking Oaks victory.

"We gave her a mid-season break after she'd coughed for a short time," Candy recalls. "The Oaks was a bit of a shot in the dark because she was by the sprinter Saritamer, but she was a very tough filly who took an awful lot of work. Her homework was always absolutely electric."

Time Charter's exploits must be seen in the context of the era. In her time there wasn't a single Group 1 race in Britain for older fillies and mares, which meant that the best fillies were invariably retired after their three-year-old campaigns. Only those of Time Charter's exceptional quality could prosper thereafter.
JULIAN MUSCAT

**Foaled**
April 6, 1979
**Pedigree**
Saritamer – Centrocon
**Breeders**
W and R Barnett
**Owner**
Robert Barnett
**Trainer**
Henry Candy
**Main jockeys**
Billy Newnes
and Joe Mercer
**Career record**
Nine wins and seven places from 20 runs
**Most famous for**
Winning Group 1 races at 3, 4 and 5
**Fate at stud**
Dam of ten foals and seven winners, among them Zinaad and Time Allowed, both winners of the Gr 2 Jockey Club Stakes

# 38

# DANEDREAM

The racing career of Danedream was a German fairytale to rival Hansel and Gretel, albeit one without the requisite happy ending. It is the story of a small, undistinguished-looking filly sold for a song who went on to become one of the best horses in the world before she was retired to the paddocks in freakish circumstances.

Danedream, the little filly with the big heart, was purchased for €9,000 as a two-year-old by owner Heiko Volz, a furniture manufacturer with just five horses in training under the stable name Gestut Burg Eberstein. But handsome is as handsome does and the ugly duckling turned into a swan. Having started out with a winning juvenile debut at the obscure French venue Wissembourg in Alsace in June 2010, she stunned the racing world as a three-year-old in

ON THE NOD: Danedream (near side) denies Nathaniel by a nose in a pulsating climax to the King George VI and Queen Elizabeth Stakes in July 2012 to become the first filly to win both the Ascot showpiece and the Prix de l'Arc de Triomphe

2011 with a five-length victory in record time in the Prix de l'Arc de Triomphe. She was only Germany's second winner of Europe's showpiece contest after the shock 1975 victor Star Appeal.

Danedream was not done there either. In the summer of her four-year-old campaign she became the first filly ever to win both the Arc and the King George with a gutsy last-gasp success at Ascot, one of five Group 1 triumphs on a CV also featuring two runnings of Germany's most prestigious race, the Grosser Preis von Baden. She was named Germany's Horse of the Year in both 2011 and 2012. But her career was to end when she was denied the chance to defend her title in the Arc owing to an outbreak of swamp fever at her Cologne training centre.

"I have had a lot of Group 1 winners but it is easy to say Danedream is the best," said trainer Peter Schiergen, a five-time champion jockey before becoming a trainer. "The Arc was crazy and the King George was the same. She was a lovely filly and she will never be forgotten."

Beaten on six of her first seven starts – one via disqualification, admittedly – it was not until Danedream was stepped up in trip as a three-year-old that her supreme ability really started to show. Yet despite pummelling her rivals in the Grade 2 Oaks d'Italia and a pair of German Group 1s, notably a six-length drubbing of a good field at Baden-Baden, Danedream was still a relatively unknown quantity on Europe's major racing stages, which explains how she was sent off a 20-1 outsider in a 16-runner field at Longchamp. There was no quibbling with her performance there, however: settled in midfield by jockey Andrasch Starke, she moved through strongly to take the lead in the straight before pulling away to score by five lengths from Shareta. Among those further back were Snow Fairy, So You Think and St Nicholas Abbey.

"My father has had horses for 35 years but we have never had anything like this," said Volz, whose family sold a half-share in Danedream to Japanese breeding giant Teruya Yoshida before the Arc. "We bought her at the breeze-up sale and we just thought she would be a fun horse who could maybe win a race. She has just improved and improved."

A second Arc would be the primary target of Danedream's four-year-old campaign; in the event, her 2011 season was to contain a notable highlight – just not in France. She touched off the previous year's winner Nathaniel to become the first German horse to claim the King George, and the first filly to win both the Arc and the Ascot showpiece.

After a workmanlike victory in the Grosser Preis von Baden (where she was unsuited by the slow pace), Danedream looked fully primed for a return visit to Longchamp, but it wasn't to be. All 300 horses at her Cologne training centre were put under quarantine restrictions when a horse tested positive for equine infectious anaemia, more commonly known as swamp fever and often fatal to horses. Although Danedream herself was entirely unaffected, the filly was not allowed to leave; she was soon retired bred to Frankel.

"As a jockey I know I will never get a filly like her again," said Starke. "German racing will never get a filly like her again, not after what happened in the Arc and the King George. She was the horse of a lifetime to me." **NICHOLAS GODFREY**

**Foaled**
May 7, 2008
**Pedigree**
Lomitas – Danedrop
**Breeder**
Gestut Brummerhof
**Owners**
Gestut Burg Eberstein and Teruya Yoshida
**Trainer**
Peter Schiergen
**Main jockey**
Andrasch Starke
**Career record**
Eight wins and four places from 17 runs
**Most famous for**
One of the best racehorses in German racing history, won the Arc in record time before landing the King George as a four-year-old; five Group 1 wins altogether
**Fate at stud**
Produced three foals (two by Frankel, eldest of which is an unraced three-year-old called Nothing But Dreams with Roger Varian); also yearling colt by Dubawi; covered again by Frankel last year

"The Arc was crazy and the King George was the same. She was a lovely filly and she will never be forgotten"

# 39

# LOCHSONG

**Foaled**
April 26, 1988
**Pedigree**
Song – Peckitts Well
**Breeder**
Littleton Stud
**Owner**
Jeff Smith
**Trainer**
Ian Balding
**Main jockeys**
Frankie Dettori
and Willie Carson
**Career record**
15 wins and six places
from 27 runs
**Most famous for**
Spellbinding speed that
earned her Horse of the
Year honours
**Fate at stud**
Had seven offspring who
raced, the best of them
being Diadem Stakes
third Lochridge

HAPPY GIRL: Lochsong
with trainer Ian Balding
(left), jockey Frankie
Dettori (centre) and owner
Jeff Smith in the winner's
enclosure after the
Nunthorpe Stakes at York
in August 1993

Speed thrills, and Lochsong had speed. She was prone to use it early and generously, like a factory worker on a Friday night with his weekly pay packet clutched in his fist, yet there was always enough in hand to see her safely through the five furlongs. But for such a fast mover, she started out awfully slowly.

"The thing about Lochsong was that she came out of nowhere," said Ian Balding. Lochsong was never the soundest of horses, had joints to make a vet shake his head in despair, didn't make it to the racecourse until the August of her three-year-old career, a career that fell neatly into two halves. At the age of four, a little like magic, she blossomed and bore fruit. Handicaps first, the world later.

The sprint handicap division is probably the most competitive in the sport, heavily subscribed, fiercely contended, prone to the handicapper's whim. To cut a swathe of glory through the great, historic six-furlong contests in summer and autumn is nigh impossible, but in 1992 Lochsong made it look almost straightforward. Fourth place in the Wokingham was the sniper's warning shot, sufficient to calibrate the sights. Thereafter, she never missed.

The Stewards' Cup, the Portland, the Ayr Gold Cup, as easy as one-two-three yet so difficult that no other horse had ever done the treble. At Doncaster she made all, at Ayr she made all on her side of the track, her tearaway tactics helping to cement her place in the public's affections, for a front-runner's perceived vulnerability is an endearing thing. Off she'd go from the cannon's mouth of the starting stalls, explosive, exciting, exceptional. But by now, of course, handicaps were too small a sphere to contain her.

It was a decent era for sprinters and at first Lochsong could only get a toehold on the ladder.

The electrifying speed that lit up her passage through the ranks was, in higher grade, only 40-watt stuff. She struggled with the transition until, one day at Goodwood, when the downhill track lent her wings in the Group 3 King George Stakes, the lights came on. She beat fellow trailblazer Paris House by a head, and the good times started again.

Her next outing was her first in Group 1 company, the Nunthorpe Stakes at York, and on form she couldn't beat Paris House. Lochsong was never one for doing things by the book, mind.

"She was a fairytale – she had shocking joints and we were just hoping she could win a small race," said

> "She was a fairytale – she had shocking joints and we were just hoping she could win a small race"

Jeff Smith. "My favourite memory is her Nunthorpe win – on the form book she couldn't win and I wasn't confident at all, but she was a revelation at York. She blew them away inside the first furlong. I've never been so shocked or so pleasantly surprised."

She blew everyone away. She left them standing at the stalls, then quickened again a furlong out to set the seal on her transformation. A little over 12 months earlier she had won the Stewards' Cup off a mark of 82, now she was champion sprinter-elect. Weeks later, in the cloying Longchamp mud, she put both hands on the crown with a six-length demolition job in the Prix de l'Abbaye. Few have gone so far and so fast as Lochsong.

She was often unstoppable but never unbeatable – she couldn't make it pay over six furlongs at the top level, she had a dash of temperament that saw her lose the chance of a second Nunthorpe on the way to the start, and she lost more Group 1s than she won – but no-one minded that, it was all part of her considerable charm.

European Horse of the Year in 1993, twice European champion sprinter, five-length winner of the (then Group 2) King's Stand Stakes and another Abbaye at the age of six, the horse Frankie Dettori credits with putting him on the map – Lochsong was all of these and something more as well. She was such fun. **STEVE DENNIS**

FLYING MACHINE:
Lochsong wins the Prix
de l'Abbaye at Longchamp
in 1994 for the second
year running under
Frankie Dettori

IN COMMAND: Lochsong
pulls clear of her rivals for
a five-length victory in the
King's Stand Stakes at Royal
Ascot in June 1994

JOB DONE: Frankie Dettori is congratulated by trainer Ian Balding after success in the 1994 Prix de l'Abbaye

# 40

# RACHEL ALEXANDRA

America's Sweetheart she may have been, but in compiling probably the greatest campaign by a three-year-old filly in US racing history, Rachel Alexandra earned enduring fame well beyond her national boundaries.

The bay filly with the distinctive white blaze was unbeaten in eight starts at seven different tracks in 2009, often trouncing her rivals by football-pitch margins. Rachel Alexandra beat the boys three times in 2009, all of them in Grade 1 company, starting with the Preakness Stakes, where she became the first of her sex to win the second leg of the Triple Crown for 85 years. Such was the towering nature of her achievements that she was voted a clearcut winner of the Horse of the Year ballot at the Eclipse Awards for 2009 ahead of the West Coast giant Zenyatta.

Named after her original owner-breeder Dolphus Morrison's granddaughter, Rachel Alexandra was trained initially by little-known Hal Wiggins, for whom she won three of her six races as a two-year-old.

With Calvin Borel as her regular partner, the filly easily won her first three starts as a three-year-old before a truly staggering performance in the Kentucky Oaks that confirmed her superstar status. After stalking the pace, she galloped further and further away to finish entirely on her own, scoring by more than 20 lengths in a display of complete authority. Four days later it was announced Rachel Alexandra had been sold to billionaire Jess Jackson's Stonestreet Stables in a deal said to be worth $10 million. "The story of this filly is still being written," said Jackson, who transferred her to Steve Asmussen.

Targets were realigned in ambitious fashion: Rachel Alexandra was supplemented at a cost of $100,000 to the Preakness Stakes, where she cleared away at the head of the stretch before holding the late rally of Kentucky Derby winner Mine That Bird by a length. No filly had won since Nellie Morse in 1924.

Only two rivals dared to take her on as she returned to her own sex in the Mother Goose at Belmont, where she was sent off a 1-20 shot and duly won by more than 19 lengths before another blockbuster performance ensued as she overwhelmed a top-class field in the $1.25m Haskell; six lengths adrift in second was Belmont Stakes winner Summer Bird.

The filly's celebrity status with the wider public had long since been confirmed. "I can't tell you how amazing it is that everybody asks me about Rachel," said Asmussen. "I think it's fantastic – and I think Rachel is very deserving of the admiration. I can't remember the last little girl I've met that didn't ask me how Rachel was doing."

She raced just once more in 2009, this time beating older males in the Grade 1 Woodward Stakes at Saratoga, where she needed every ounce of courage to hold the late-running Macho Again as the roof was lifted off the Saratoga stands. She had won her eight starts in 2009 by a cumulative 65 lengths.

An intense rivalry had developed over the course of the year between supporters of Rachel Alexandra and Californian queen Zenyatta, busily compiling her own unblemished record. Rachel Alexandra's connections declined to run her in the Breeders' Cup owing to the artificial surface at Santa Anita, where Zenyatta duly produced a breathtaking display to win the Classic. Battle lines were drawn in a textbook east-versus-west rivalry in the Horse of the Year ballot; Rachel Alexandra triumphed with 130 votes compared to her rival's 99.

Rachel Alexandra was never to reach the same heights as a four-year-old in 2010, when she was beaten in three of five starts and failed to add to her Grade 1 tally. After another below-par effort at Saratoga in August she was retired to the paddocks. "As a three-year-old she set standards and records that no filly before her ever achieved – I suspect it will be quite a while before a three-year-old filly ever equals or surpasses those achievements," said Jackson, who died of cancer in April 2011.

Asmussen added: "I have been blessed to have been part of history. The fans adored her, we all did." She never did meet Zenyatta.

NICHOLAS GODFREY

**Foaled**
January 29, 2006
**Pedigree**
Medaglia d'Oro –
Lotta Kim
**Breeder**
Dolphus C Morrison
**Owners**
Stonestreet Stables LLC
and Harold McCormick
**Trainers**
Steve Asmussen and
Hal Wiggins
**Main jockey**
Calvin Borel
**Career record**
13 wins and five places
from 19 runs
**Most famous for**
Unbeaten in eight
races in spectacular
three-year-old campaign
in 2009 when she
beat males three
times (including in the
Preakness Stakes) and
became North American
Horse of the Year
**Fate at stud**
Produced only two
foals as broodmare
and not bred since
difficult delivery of
subsequent Grade 1
winner Rachel's Valentina
and serious post-foaling
medical scare

**HOME LIFE:** History-maker Rachel Alexandra at Stonestreet Stables in January 2012 following a career which saw her become the first of her sex to win the Preakness Stakes – the second leg of the US Triple Crown – in 85 years

**"I have been blessed to have been part of history. The fans adored her, we all did"**

# 41

# ANNIE POWER

Annie Power, whose career was marked not only by its brilliance but also a touch of drama, can be considered one of the top female hurdlers of all time.

Her record suggests she was nearly impossible to beat when she stood up: in 16 completed starts, she won 15, with the emphatic 2016 Champion Hurdle victory the obvious highlight. However, a memorable all-the-way victory was a far cry from her Cheltenham experience the previous season, when she came down at the last in the OLBG Mares' Hurdle. Bookmakers claimed the fall saved them a £60 million payout.

Named after her breeder Eamon Cleary's grandmother, Annie Power has always an exalted reputa-

**LAUGHING MATTER:**
Annie Power with her happy connections after she landed the 2016 Champion Hurdle at Cheltenham 12 months on from her final-flight fall in the Mares' Hurdle

tion, right back to the days when she started out in bumpers in August 2012 ridden by the amateur Patrick Mullins. She won three in quick succession, with the first two for Jim Bolger before she was transferred to Mullins' father Willie.

Annie Power then progressed to land four mares' novice hurdles that same campaign, culminating in a Fairyhouse Grade 1 at the Irish Grand National meeting after which Willie Mullins could hardly contain his enthusiasm. "She could be anything," he told reporters at the track. "She's starting to show you guys now what I always knew she was."

By now Ruby Walsh had taken over riding duties from Mullins jnr, and Annie Power had been pur-

## "It was fantastic for her to win at Cheltenham at the third attempt"

**Foaled**
March 20, 2008
**Pedigree**
Shirocco – Anno Luce
**Breeder**
Eamon Cleary
**Owner**
Susannah Ricci
**Trainers**
Jim Bolger and Willie Mullins
**Main jockey**
Ruby Walsh
**Career record**
15 wins and one place from 17 runs
**Most famous for**
Top-class hurdling mare who registered dominant Champion Hurdle triumph in 2016 at Cheltenham, where she had crashed out in mares' race 12 months earlier
**Fate at stud**
In foal to Camelot in the spring of 2017

chased by Rich and Susannah Ricci. Few horses have carried the famous pink and green silks with such prowess. She ran five times in 2013–14, confirming her supreme ability with easy victories in England – at Ascot, Cheltenham and Doncaster – that extended her unbeaten run to ten. But she came unstuck for the first time at Cheltenham, where she was favourite for the World Hurdle, going down in the closing stages to a stronger stayer in More Of That. Dropped back in trip, another Grade 1 success at Punchestown against her own sex was little more than a formality.

She was unseen in public until her fateful visit to the Cheltenham Festival in 2015, where she was odds-on to follow standing dish Quevega in the OLBG Mares' Hurdle. Mullins had been imperious on the first-day card, where Walsh partnered Douvan, Un De Sceaux and Faugheen to a Grade 1 treble, each of them backed as if defeat was out of the question before a notorious twist of fate. Annie Power cruised around the inner before going on two out with the race in safe-keeping – only to dive at the last and hit the turf with a thud that produced an audible gasp from the stands and sighs of relief from bookmakers facing massive liabilities on the four-timer.

Annie Power's complete superiority over her fellow mares was demonstrated with a ten-length victory at Punchestown, where she was to score on her reappearance in February 2016 after another lengthy absence. Next came Cheltenham, where she was parachuted into the Champion Hurdle when her stablemate Faugheen, the defending champion, got injured. This was quite some animal to have sitting on the bench: Annie Power was sent off 5-2 favourite and duly claimed the championship with an accomplished performance under Walsh, who took few prisoners by kicking her straight into the lead and staying there. She drew away approaching the second-last and stayed on strongly to win by four and a half lengths from My Tent Or Yours to become the first mare to win the Champion for two decades.

After destroying her Aintree Hurdle rivals, Annie Power was put away again but failed to grace to racecourse again due to injury. Mullins says: "It was fantastic for her to win at Cheltenham at the third attempt. We had no real concerns about her dropping in distance and she showed the combination of speed and stamina we knew she possessed."
NICHOLAS GODFREY

MORNING WORKOUT:
Annie Power and Sonny
Carey on the gallops at
Cheltenham two days
before the 2016 Champion
Hurdle

LEAP OF FAITH: Annie
Power clears the final flight
before going on to win the
2016 Aintree Hurdle by
18 lengths from My Tent
Or Yours

COSTLY MISTAKE: Annie
Power and Ruby Walsh
crash to the floor after
falling at the final flight in
the 2015 Mares' Hurdle at
Cheltenham. Bookmakers
claimed the fall saved them
a £60 million payout

# 42

## USER FRIENDLY

Making her debut as a three-year-old in a Class 6 Sandown maiden, User Friendly might be said to have slipped in under the radar as she romped home a 25-1 winner, but it was the last time she was ever underestimated on the track.

As a daughter of the 1985 Derby hero Slip Anchor and winning Blakeney mare Rostova, the Bill Gredley homebred was always likely to be a slow-burning stayer with a touch of class, but by the time she made off with the 1992 Lingfield Oaks Trial on her second start it was plain she was ready to fulfil her destiny sooner rather than later.

"We sent her back to Stetchworth Stud when she first arrived," recalls her trainer Clive Brittain, "but they did such a good job with her that three weeks after she came back she did a canter round Waterhall and it was as if she hadn't missed a day's work.

"Before her second canter, I told Michael Roberts we might have something a bit special and when he got off her he said to me 'she's all class', so that's how we treated her from then on.

"Unluckily for Michael, Sir Henry [Cecil] had asked him to ride the favourite at Sandown; I warned him that if he got off mine, the owner wasn't the kind that would let him back on, and he made a costly decision."

Launched into top company on the strength of her Lingfield success, she was outpointed in the Oaks market by red-hot 11-10 favourite All At Sea, but once in full stride up the Epsom straight had far too much for the Cecil-trained filly and, kicking on fully three furlongs from home under the ever-present George Duffield, stretched clear to score by three and a half lengths, with 20 lengths back to the third.

"I think that was her finest performance," says

**Foaled**
February 4, 1989
**Pedigree**
Slip Anchor – Rostova
**Breeder**
Stetchworth Park Stud
**Owner**
Bill Gredley
**Trainer**
Clive Brittain
**Main jockey**
George Duffield
**Career record**
Eight wins and two places from 15 runs
**Most famous for**
An unbeaten run of six races to open her career, encompassing three Oaks and a St Leger
**Fate at stud**
No stars among her eight foals, although Two Miles West, a son of Sadler's Wells, won once on the Flat for Aidan O'Brien and seven times over hurdles and fences for Jonjo O'Neill, while Downtown landed a Group 3 at Cork for David Wachman

Brittain. "After Lingfield I'd said to Bill that unless I made a mistake she wouldn't get beaten that year, and I wasn't far wrong."

It was the start of a summer spree that encompassed three more Group 1 successes, the next being the Irish Oaks in which, although sent off the 8-11 favourite, she had to battle hard to see off second favourite Market Booster by a neck.

Again starting at 8-11, she duly added the Yorkshire Oaks to her portfolio, but it was in the St Leger on her next start that she made her indelible mark on turf history, travelling smoothly throughout before being unleashed at the two-furlong pole and rolling into a lead that grew and grew.

AT FULL STRETCH:
User Friendly gallops
to a two-and-a-half-length
victory in the Yorkshire
Oaks in August 1992 two
months after her success
in the Oaks at Epsom and
a month before landing the
St Leger at Doncaster

"She went from being a filly you might win a Yarmouth maiden with to one ending up winning five Group 1s. She was something special"

Steve Cauthen gave game chase on the John Gosden-trained Sonus but couldn't get any closer than three and a half lengths, with Frankie Dettori a further neck behind on second favourite Bonny Scot.

In truth, they were bit-part players in a drama dominated by the European Horse of the Year, who was pipped by Subotica on soft ground in the Arc but then flopped in the Japan Cup. "It was the only mistake I made with her," says Brittain. "Just one race too many. George says she should never have been beaten in the Arc and if she'd won the Arc she wouldn't have gone to Japan.

"But she went from being a filly you might win a Yarmouth maiden with to one ending up winning five Group 1s. She was something special – I rode her myself a couple of times and she was surprisingly light-footed for a big filly and never gave you the impression she was struggling."

The following season User Friendly won the Grand Prix de Saint-Cloud, but that was the only time she got her head in front until she headed to America to be trained by Rodney Rash as a five-year-old, having been trounced in heavy ground in the Arc.

In the States she scored once at Del Mar under Chris Antley, but these were mere footnotes to a romp of four consecutive Group 1s in her Classic season that remain etched in the consciousness.

PETER THOMAS

# 43

# IN THE GROOVE

As the two-year-old In The Groove was taking her first steps towards a career on the racecourse, David Elsworth was putting the finishing touches to Desert Orchid's preparations for the 1989 Cheltenham Gold Cup.

The master dual-purpose trainer might have been forgiven for being distracted, but by the end of the Flat season he had on his hands a filly who, for all that her record contained just one win from four starts, was primed for great things.

Her victory had come in the Moorestyle Convivial Maiden at York and had been followed by defeat in Group company at Phoenix Park, but the finished three-year-old article was a different beast.

BATTLE ROYAL: In The Groove (near side) makes a winning return from Zoman in the Trusthouse Forte Mile at Sandown in April 1991 in the hands of Steve Cauthen

**Foaled**
February 25, 1987
**Pedigree**
Night Shift – Pine Ridge I
**Breeder**
Capt John Macdonald
Buchanan
**Owner**
Brian Cooper
**Trainer**
David Elsworth
**Career record**
Seven wins and eight
places from 21 runs
**Most famous for**
A Guineas, a Juddmonte
International and a
Champion Stakes in the
glorious summer of 1990
**Fate at stud**
None of her seven foals
came close to matching
her ability, but
Incarvillea, a daughter
of Mr Prospector, won
a Newmarket maiden
and a Pontefract condi-
tions race on her only
two starts for
David Loder

"We bought her at David's Christmas party," re-calls owner Brian Cooper, "and we always knew she was no forlorn hope because he had Dead Certain in the yard at the time, who went on to win the Lowther and the Cheveley Park, and they worked together on a few occasions.

"Her runs at two didn't stand out but I'd say her best performance visually was the Irish 1,000 Guineas, which was an enormous high."

The daughter of Night Shift had limbered up with a close second to Heart Of Joy in the Nell Gwyn and a down-the-field run in Salsabil's Newmarket Guin-eas, but then hit her stride with victory over Sarde-gna in the Musidora, followed by a three-length

thrashing of Heart Of Joy in the Irish Guineas.

The Curragh performance was a pitch-perfect example of the running style that served In The Groove so well. With Steve Cauthen settling her quietly in rear, she made stealthy ground down the wide outside before unleashing a withering chal-lenge that was all too much for the narrow Guineas runner-up and 4-6 favourite.

It was a flawless demonstration of raw speed channelled to the sharp end of a Group 1 race, giving Elsworth his first Classic success and teeing up a breathtaking summer to come.

After enduring an interrupted run under Cash Asmussen in fourth place behind Salsabil in the Oaks, the imposing bay travelled to York after a ten-week break.

Such was the strength of the field in the Judd-monte International she was sent off only third favourite, but the ten-furlong trip and good ground proved her optimum and allowed her to produce perhaps the defining performance of her career against all-comers.

Reunited with regular partner Cauthen, she was anchored amenably at the back of the nine-strong field, sweeping into the front rank over a furlong from home as Eclipse winner Elmaamul and the fancied four-year-old Batshoof fought for room. Running on strongly, she held that pair by a length and a half and two and a half lengths.

It was In The Groove at her simple, clinical best, showing devastating pace that overwhelmed a top-class field.

"She wasn't terribly big, but she had such a strong frame and was very broad in the chest and she had a head on her like a JCB," remembers Cooper. Elsworth says by way of clarification, "but she needed to be strong that day. I'd say she was the best filly I ever had".

Cooper adds: "Although she wasn't a homebred and we didn't know her as well as we knew some of our others, she had a good temperament, a won-derful turn of foot and tried really hard. She was a joy to own."

After finding her stamina stretched in the Prix de l'Arc de Triomphe, In The Groove went on to outgun Linamix, Legal Case and Elmaamul again in the Champion Stakes at Newmarket, before embarking on a four-year-old career that peaked in the Sandown Mile and over a mile and a half in the Coronation Cup.

Although that was to prove the final win of her career, her best moments live long in the memory.
PETER THOMAS

> "She had a good temperament, a wonderful turn of foot and tried really hard. She was a joy to own"

# 44

## QUEVEGA

There she was, every spring, as regular as the daffodils and as welcome. We never saw that much of Quevega – there wasn't that much to see of the little mare anyway – but her rarity value served only to underline her appeal.

After all, there aren't many horses who do something that's never been done before. Back in the sepia half-light of history Golden Miller won the Cheltenham Gold Cup five times in a row and no horse since then had taken such an iron grip on one single race at the great equinoctial gathering of the clans. Then along came Quevega, but she had wriggled her way into our hearts long before she wrote herself into the record books.

The Grade 2 David Nicholson Mares' Hurdle was a newish addition to the festival and like all newness in racing there had been concern about how it would be accepted, how it would fit in. What it needed was something to give it a place in the world and it couldn't have asked for a better advertisement than Quevega.

She was five on her first appearance at Cheltenham, owing her position as clear market leader to a strong home reputation rather than any particular brilliance on the track. She took the race apart, sprinting up the hill to win by 14 lengths, proving herself a class above her fellow distaffers and becoming an instant favourite with the public.

Quevega hadn't yet settled into her routine, though, hadn't yet honed her minimalist approach to racing into the cutting edge that would see all fall

**Foaled**
April 11, 2004
**Pedigree**
Robin Des Champs –
Vega IV
**Breeder**
Pierre Rives
**Owners**
Hammer and Trowel
Syndicate
**Trainer**
Willie Mullins
**Main jockey**
Ruby Walsh
**Career record**
16 wins and five places
from 24 runs
**Most famous for**
Winning the same race at
the Cheltenham Festival
six years running
**Fate at stud**
Has a two-year-old filly
by Beat Hollow

## "She's not just the horse of a lifetime, she's a horse of a century"

before her in the coming years. The following season saw the pattern take shape – she went to Cheltenham without a prep run, saw off her rivals with varying degrees of ease and elan, and then stopped off at Punchestown to do the same in the Grade 1 World Series Hurdle over three miles. That was that; job done; see you next year.

That was how it went for four campaigns (2010–13). Now and again at Cheltenham she took on a brief air of vulnerability, getting stuck in midfield, crowded, harried, but as soon as the field turned for home the gaps appeared and she flew through them, Ruby Walsh – who called Quevega "one of the most special women in my life", secure in the knowledge wife Gillian would understand – moving through the rush-hour traffic as easily as if he had a blue light on his helmet.

There were calls for her to run in better grade at the festival, to test her mettle against the best around as she did at Punchestown, but her connections stuck to the model that worked, the 'if-it-ain't-broke' defence, for any victory at Cheltenham is a prize beyond compare. She was perennially odds-on, everyone's banker bet, a statistician's daydream; Quevega never let anyone down.

"I grew up reading about Golden Miller and wondering how a horse could do that," says Willie Mullins, whose brilliance in getting Quevega to the festival six years in a row – five times without a prep run – should never be underestimated.

"I never dreamed I would even come near to one, let alone train one. She's not just the horse of a lifetime, she's a horse of a century. She's so precious and we're so lucky to have had her."

In 2014, at the age of ten, she came for the final time, her sixth victory in sight. Again there was the frisson of will-she-won't-she when stablemate Glens Melody went clear in a bid to spoil the party, but Walsh finally got the flame to catch halfway up the run-in and the grandstands went up in unison.

She caught Glens Melody, of course she did. She passed her, took command as bedlam broke out all around, won by a comfortable three-quarters of a length. And she passed Golden Miller too.

In the newsrooms of two nations the headline writers dusted off the old standby 'The Joy of Six' to encapsulate the event. Six wins in a row – what a remarkable horse Quevega was and what joy she gave.

STEVE DENNIS

**LEAP TO GLORY:**
Quevega and Ruby Walsh
clear the last to win a sixth
consecutive Mares' Hurdle
in 2014

ONE LOVE: Ruby Walsh casts an admiring glance at Quevega after his partner won a sixth Mares' Hurdle

STAR ATTRACTION: Quevega returns to the winner's enclosure after making history at Cheltenham

NEW LIFE: Quevega at the Irish National Stud in January 2017

# 45
# ENABLE

Aunt Edith, Park Top, Dahlia, Pawneese, Time Charter, Danedream, Taghrooda. It's an elite, exclusive club, and its membership was swelled when Enable became the eighth filly or mare to win the King George VI and Queen Elizabeth Stakes, British racing's midsummer highlight.

It's a club any female can join but not necessarily one they'll look wholly at home in, but when Enable made light of the soft ground and the strong opposition at Ascot she stamped herself as a filly of the highest class and the de facto leader of the European middle-distance division for 2017. It was a superlative performance, flashing through the rain to beat Eclipse winner Ulysses by four and a half lengths, and one that augured even greater things to come.

It wasn't necessarily planned like that, however. If there was a star in the making in the frequently influential conditions race at Newbury in April it was expected to be her stablemate Shutter Speed, who backed up a burgeoning reputation with a comfortable success. Enable, beneath the green second-string cap of her owner Khalid Abdullah, was a promising third, just a good-looking bridesmaid carrying the train of a ravishing bride. Funny old game, racing.

Shutter Speed won the Musidora at York but was only fourth in the Prix de Diane; Enable won the Cheshire Oaks and then began her rapid ascent to the summit, passing her stablemate on the way with barely a backward glance.

Her proven stamina gave her sturdy credentials in the Oaks, but all the newsprint was about odds-on favourite Rhododendron, who was considered a little unlucky when runner-up in the 1,000 Guineas and expected to make amends at Epsom.

Her stamina had to be taken on trust, and it would be an inflexible judge who said she hadn't stayed. Rhododendron was six lengths clear of the third horse; trouble was, Enable was five lengths further up the track.

In a race run in a brief and vicious thunderstorm, Enable was lightning in a bottle. She and Rhododendron went clear of their rivals three furlongs from home, the race a thrilling match that swiftly fizzled out as Enable dropped her as nonchalantly as the yellow jersey drops his domestiques on some awful Alpine climb. Her superiority was plain; here was a new star and, considering the muddling result of the Derby 24 hours later, possibly the brightest of all the three-year-olds.

SINGING IN THE RAIN: Frankie Dettori can't hide his delight after Enable completes a stunning triumph in the King George VI & Queen Elizabeth Stakes at Ascot in July 2017

**Foaled**
February 12, 2014
**Pedigree**
Nathaniel ~ Concentric
**Breeder**
Juddmonte Farms Ltd
**Owner**
Khalid Abdullah
**Trainer**
John Gosden
**Main jockey**
Frankie Dettori
**Career Record**
Five wins and one place
from six runs
**Most famous for**
Being a rare female
winner of the King
George VI and Queen
Elizabeth Stakes

The Irish Oaks was the obvious sequel and at 2-5 Enable the obvious winner. The result was no surprise but the manner of victory took the breath away – again Enable drew easily clear of her rivals, bouncing off the fast ground, being eased in the closing stages but still five and a half lengths clear of Rain Goddess at the line. If there is one thing that impresses ratings experts – actually there are two, but top-rank horses don't tend to concede lumps of weight any more – it is a wide-margin success, and Enable had just posted two of them in Classics.

Two weeks later, mirroring the career arc of the great Dahlia, who had only a week to spare between the Irish Oaks and her first King George, she ticked off the requirements that vouchsafe entry into the foyer of the Pantheon – she beat colts, she beat older horses, she won an all-aged major Group 1 in captivating style. Here was the heiress of the ages.

"She's very good, she's a superstar," said a hungry Frankie Dettori, who had starved himself to make the weight. "The best filly I've trained," said veteran John Gosden, shuffling a personal pack including Royal Heroine, Ryafan, The Fugue, Dar Re Mi and Taghrooda. "I think this is the best filly we've ever had," said the owner's son Prince Ahmed Bin Khalid.

No filly or mare has ever won the King George and Prix de l'Arc de Triomphe in the same year. Enable may yet find herself in a much more exclusive club.
STEVE DENNIS

> "She's very
> good, she's
> a superstar"

JUMPING FOR JOY: Frankie Dettori performs his familiar flying dismount from Enable after the filly's record-breaking Oaks success at Epsom in June 2017

ONE HORSE IN IT: Enable and Frankie Dettori storm clear of Rhododendron to land the Oaks at Epsom in June 2017

MUDDY MARVEL: Muddy Marvel: Frankie Dettori (pink cap) and Enable go clear in the King George as they run on to complete a four-and-a-half-length success over Ulysses (second right), with Idaho (striped cap) in third at Ascot in July 2017

# 46

# URBAN SEA

Urban Sea was a dangerous lady to trifle with. Dismissed as a 37-1 chance for the Prix de l'Arc de Triomphe, she confounded the experts by making off with Europe's middle-distance championship. And when that 1993 renewal was dismissed as sub-standard, Urban Sea extracted revenge by breeding one of the finest Arc winners the race has seen.

Sea The Stars would have made any mother proud. His 2009 Arc triumph completed a unique sweep of six Group 1 races in his sophomore campaign, yet even he cannot hope to generate as much fame as his celebrated half-brother. In Galileo, Urban Sea produced the defining thoroughbred of the 21st century to date. The accolade will almost certainly hold true at the millennium's close.

Trained as part of a mixed string by now-retired Jean Lesbordes in France, Urban Sea continues to rewrite records. She is one of only two mares to have bred a pair of Derby winners, one of two Arc winners to have bred an Arc winner, and the only mare to have produced separate winners of both races. It is not the sort of legacy you'd expect from a yearling filly who cost just Fr280,000 (about £30,000) in 1990.

---

**"She is one of only two mares to have bred a pair of Derby winners, one of two Arc winners to have bred an Arc winner, and the only mare to have produced separate winners of both races"**

In truth, there was little to foreshadow what Urban Sea would achieve until she contested that Arc. She had ability, sure, but in a 23-strong field she did not feature among 15 individual Group 1 winners to assemble at Longchamp.

It helped that the four-year-old was always well placed in a race run at a slow tempo on testing ground. And she benefited from the wayward antics of Talloires, another horse bred by Marystead Farm, a Kentucky-based venture involving some of France's leading breeders.

Talloires swerved both left and right down the Longchamp straight, in the process hampering some rivals while forcing others into evasive action. In the latter category was White Muzzle, whom John Reid brought with a late run as Urban Sea finally mastered Opera House inside the final furlong. Much to the chagrin of his trainer Peter Chapple-Hyam, White Muzzle finished fast but to no avail. Urban Sea repelled him by a neck.

Urban Sea came into the Arc in the form of her life. She was winning for the fourth time that season – on the second occasion she won at the provincial venue of Le Lion d'Angers. What characterised her to that point was her affinity for travelling. She'd run with merit in Germany, Hong Kong and Britain before she won the Arc, although she could finish only eighth on a subsequent assignment in the Japan Cup.

Urban Sea ran in the silks of David Tsui, who initially campaigned her with some associates. She might easily have won the Arc for somebody else, since she was offered at the Goffs Arc Sale the previous year to dissolve the partnership. Fortunately for Tsui, he had the final word at Fr3 million (£320,000) and assumed sole ownership.

Lady Luck thus smiled on the family, as David's son Christopher later acknowledged. "Urban Sea was a member of our family for 20 years," he says. "She was a wonderful racemare and an even greater broodmare.

"What would racing be like today if my mother [Ling] hadn't made the decisions she did with Urban Sea? She received so many offers after Urban Sea won the Arc. If she had accepted any of them the entire European racing scene would be completely different."

That latter sentiment does not incline towards exaggeration. Galileo has been leading sire in Britain and Ireland seven times, while Sea The Stars sired his first Derby winner Harzand earlier this year. It's a legacy that promises to run and run.
JULIAN MUSCAT

**Foaled**
February 18, 1989
**Pedigree**
Miswaki – Allegretta
**Breeder**
Marystead Farm, USA
**Owner**
David Tsui
**Trainer**
Jean Lesbordes
**Main jockeys**
Eric Saint-Martin
and Mathieu Boutin
**Career record**
Seven wins and five places from 18 runs
**Most famous for**
Winning the 1993 Prix de l'Arc de Triomphe
**Fate at stud**
Dam of nine foals to race and eight winners, including Galileo (Derby, Irish Derby, King George; champion sire eight times), Sea The Stars (2,000 Guineas, Derby, Eclipse, Juddmonte International, Irish Champion, Prix de l'Arc de Triomphe), Black Sam Bellamy (G1), My Typhoon (G1), Melikah (runner-up in Oaks), All Too Beautiful (runner-up in Oaks), et al.

**STANDING PROUD:**
Urban Sea with trainer Jean Lesbordes after the 1993 Prix de l'Arc de Triomphe at Longchamp

# 47

## SOLERINA

👑

**Foaled**
May 10, 1997
**Pedigree**
Toulon – Deep Peace
**Breeder**
Michael J Bowe
**Owner**
John P Bowe
**Trainer**
James Bowe
**Main jockey**
Gary Hutchinson
**Career record**
22 winsand six places
from 40 runs
**Most famous for**
Winning three
consecutive runnings
(2003–05) of the
Hatton's Grace Hurdle
at Fairyhouse
**Fate at stud**
Nowhere near as prolific
in her second career as
a broodmare. Retired in
2006 to take up duties
at the Bowe family's yard,
she has bred only one
winner to date with just
three of her progeny
making the track

She might have done less homework than an ex-pelled pupil but when it came to an examination of her credentials on the track few mares made the grade like Solerina.

The diminutive scrapper went about her business with ruthless efficiency, jumping her rivals into sub-mission from the front to pass the post first in just over half her 40 starts, including 13 at Graded level.

Hailing from the Bowe family's farm, Solerina started to flourish at a time when the small-scale operation's once-in-a-lifetime horse Limestone Lad was reaching the end of his incredible career.

"She had a lot of the same characteristics as Limestone Lad even though they were from differ-ent families," says Michael Bowe, who bred the brilliant mare and assisted his late father James during the stable's golden years before taking over the reins himself in 2007.

"I always compared her to a child genius as she didn't like doing her homework at all and didn't need to as, like a lot of the good ones, she just per-formed on the track.

"The secret to training her was not to train her – you had to trust her on the day and she generally came out on top."

Owned by Bowe's brother John, Solerina, who won three times on the Flat and collected £466,471 in total earnings, showed a bit of promise in bump-ers but it wasn't until tackling hurdles she revealed the true level of her ability.

After winning her first start over hurdles, she overcame a defeat by Pizarro to rack up six victo-ries in a row, including the Future Champions Nov-ice Hurdle and Deloitte and Touche Novice Hurdle, which became the first of her five Grade 1 wins.

Much to the chagrin and perplexity of their con-

**FINE LEAP: Solerina clears a flight of hurdles on her way to winning the Tara Hurdle at Navan in December 2003**

nections, future greats such as Kicking King and Hardy Eustace had been vanquished by the minus-cule mare, who was nurtured so skilfully at the Bowe base 1,000 metres above sea level on Gath-abawn Hill, County Kilkenny.

"She shocked a lot of people and was a mystery mare," adds Bowe. "The key to her success was her soundness. She never took a lame step in her life and didn't get treated for anything – maybe the fact she was so slight helped as they always say the bigger the horse the bigger the problems."

In her first season outside of novice company Solerina led home stablemate Florida Coast in the Hatton's Grace Hurdle before ending the campaign with her only run outside Ireland when finishing

fourth behind Iris's Gift in the 2004 Stayers' Hurdle at the Cheltenham Festival over a trip further than ideal.

However, she preferred to be at home and the feeling was mutual as her appearances started to swell racecourse attendances by a couple of thousand as people clambered to witness the romantic story first hand.

A winner 18 times over hurdles at seven different tracks, Solerina relished the galloping nature of Navan, recording six successes from nine starts and dishing out another defeat to dual Champion Hurdle hero Hardy Eustace in the Tara Hurdle in December 2004.

She will most fondly be remembered for winning the Hatton's Grace three times in succession between 2003 and 2005 under regular partner Gary Hutchinson, in the process establishing a stranglehold for the Bowe family who had claimed the three previous runnings with Limestone Lad.

It was the last of those that sticks out as Solerina edged out Golden Cross in a thriller, with Brave Inca in third.

"Golden Cross had beaten her in the November Handicap on the Flat and she looked beaten after meeting the last all wrong – she broke the hurdle in half," says Bowe. "But she stayed on her feet and got up by a short head. She didn't have to battle very often in her races, but she did that day and really excelled."

ANDREW DIETZ

> "The key to her success was her soundness. She never took a lame step in her life and didn't get treated for anything"

# 48

## SOBA

A Record of 0-9 as a two-year-old coupled with a wilful temperament which brought with it an irrational hatred for bicycles and resentment at having a saddle put on her back was hardly a likely precursor to what followed during Soba's sensational three-year-old campaign.

Beaten off bottom weight in an Edinburgh nursery on the last of those nine outings as a juvenile, Soba was sent off at 33-1 in first-time blinkers for her seasonal reappearance in a 17-runner maiden at Thirsk in May, 1982. Leading two furlongs out, Soba drew clear to win by four lengths.

She did little else but win for the rest of the season under the masterful hand of David Chapman – who trained Soba for his sister, owner/breeder Muriel Hills – and, with future sprint king trainer Dandy Nicholls in the saddle, the upward curve to a rise of more than 4st in the handicap had begun.

Not a bad return for Hills, who sent her first broodmare to Most Secret to be covered for £350 at Easthorpe Hall Stud in what would prove to be an all-Yorkshire tale of rags to riches.

"I was very lucky because everything about her was bred on the cheap," says Hills. "The mare Mild

> ## "I was very lucky because everything about her was bred on the cheap"

Wind was a twin and they do say that, while they often don't do anything themselves, their foals do well. She was certainly an example of that.

"Mild Wind was lovely looking but small and not very interested in racing. But I bought her cheaply from my brother because I liked her and she turned out to produce a champion."

Hills says: "David wasn't a keen racer of two-year-olds and Soba wasn't pressed at all. She was sort of having a look around and getting a bit of experience as a two-year-old. We could have easily spoilt her at that stage, but at three she really blossomed."

Following the win at Thirsk, Chapman sent Soba reeling around the country as she racked up four more wins in the space of a month.

She was ante-post favourite for the Stewards' Cup at Goodwood when travelling to Ayr for the Tote Sprint Trophy in July, but suffered defeat at odds-on and returned home to Stillington a lame horse.

A back problem was diagnosed and following physiotherapy Soba was sent south to tackle the Goodwood feature under 8st 4lb, where she made light of the supposed poison of an extreme stands' side draw and led for every yard of the six furlongs in track-record time at odds of 18-1.

Hills says: The Stewards' Cup was the best day of her career and a great thrill. I have just been cleaning the cup ready for Christmas and it brings back all the memories."

Soba's climb up the racing pyramid continued as she landed Ripon's Great St Wilfrid Stakes, before stepping into Listed company at Doncaster when landing the Scarbrough Stakes.

Her only try in Group company at three ended in defeat in the Diadem Stakes, but with 11 wins from 14 outings – with Nicholls on board for every victory – her admirers were not put off and a reported bid of £500,000 was turned down as the Flat season drew to a close.

Soba put the Group-race record straight the following year at her beloved Goodwood, winning the King George Stakes in spectacular fashion.

And what further glories could have been garnered in 1983, but for the brilliance of the John Dunlop-trained Habibti, a year Soba's junior.

Four times the pair met in a succession of Group 1 races – starting with the July Cup and progressing through the Nunthorpe, the Haydock Sprint Cup and finally the Prix de l'Abbaye – and each time the result was the same: Habibti first; Soba condemned to be runner-up.

SCOTT BURTON

**Foaled**
1979
**Pedigree**
Most Secret – Mild Wind
**Breeder**
Muriel Hills
**Owner**
Muriel Hills
**Trainer**
David Chapman
**Main jockey**
David Nicholls
**Career record**
13 wins and eight places from 33 runs
**Most famous for**
Winning 11 races in 1982 including the Stewards' Cup in course-record time
**Fate at stud**
Although Soba would never produce anything of her own quality, she produced multiple winners and is an ancestress of Prix Ganay winner Dark Moondancer

**WINNER'S WALK:**
David Nicholls and Soba return after the King George Stakes at Glorious Goodwood in 1983

# 49

## WINTER

The British fascination with the weather knows no limitations, so it's been a pleasure to see Winter arrive in spring and summer. No-one would mind at all if she made her presence felt in autumn either. This Winter's tale is one of constant surprise, an ongoing reappraisal of the heights she may yet attain, this beautiful grey filly with a hide like a country landscape seen at first light. And her arrival

on the scene was sudden and unexpected, like snow falling on a sunny afternoon.

As a two-year-old in the care of David Wachman, the daughter of Galileo – who else? – showed promise but not a great deal more, the sum of her season being a victory in a Dundalk maiden. Wachman retired at the end of the year and Winter was transferred to Ballydoyle, no doubt with the simple intention of gaining black-type and becoming a worthy member of the Coolmore broodmare battalion. Her first outing in the spring – as O'Brien's fourth-string – achieved that objective, and the journey had begun. Of course she would take her chance in the 1,000 Guineas, but only to keep hot favourite Rhododendron company on the trip there and back.

But that was the day Winter arrived, with all the unflinching certainty of the clocks going back. Wayne Lordan wore the pale pink second colours of Sue Magnier, but his mount was no second fiddle. Rhododendron may have become unbalanced when push came to shove a furlong out, but Winter had come and gone by then, stretching away to win by a comfortable two lengths.

There was no fluke about it, simply a case of a filly who had taken a little time to flourish. Never-

WINTER WONDERLAND: Aidan O'Brien's superfilly strikes in the 2017 Nassau Stakes under Ryan Moore at Goodwood, beating Blond Me (black cap) and Sobetsu (blue) to add to her Group 1 victories in the 1,000 Guineas, Irish 1,000 Guineas and Coronation Stakes

**Foaled**
February 15, 2014
**Pedigree**
Galileo – Laddies
Poker Two
**Breeder**
Laddies Poker
Two Syndicate
**Owners**
Sue Magnier, Michael
Tabor and Derrick Smith
**Trainer**
Aidan O'Brien
**Main jockey**
Ryan Moore (also
Wayne Lordan)
**Career record**
Five wins and three
places from eight runs
**Most famous for**
The only filly to win
British and Irish Guineas,
Coronation Stakes and
Nassau Stakes

theless, something wins the Guineas every year and although as a litmus test for quality the race is irreproachable, it rarely confers greatness on its winners by itself alone. Other examinations must be undergone before true star quality can be admitted.

Three weeks later, Winter – now united with Ballydoyle's main jockey Ryan Moore and odds-on – ran out an easy winner of the Irish 1,000 Guineas, scampering nearly five lengths clear of stablemates Roly Poly and Hydrangea in a startling but somehow always half-expected O'Brien-trained one-two-three. The manner of victory brooked no argument, although there were those who muttered about the quality of the placed horses. Time would tell a different story; before July was out Roly Poly had become a dual Group 1 winner at a mile.

In two runs, Winter had vaulted from bit-part player to star of the show. She cemented her dominance over her division with another unflashy, untroubled success in the Coronation Stakes at Royal Ascot, the placings identical to those at the Curragh, Winter unshiftable at the head of the hierarchy. The next step was obvious, a variation on a theme, a longer trip, older horses, a more exacting test.

Winter came through it in her habitually imperturbable style, a filly who will never draw gasps from the crowd for audacious brilliance but will instead earn a great rumble of approval for efficiency and reliability. It was a wintry Goodwood that hosted the Nassau, the ground a morass, Winter's unproven stamina in greater question, but she barely turned an elegant grey hair in easing to victory, her progress towards super-stardom unbroken – four runs, four Group 1s, four wins.

The retirement of her stablemate Minding leaves room at the top that Winter is eminently eligible to fill, and she has been mentioned in connection with everything bar the Boat Race, with the Prix de l'Arc de Triomphe near the top of the list. She will have to beat colts if she is to raise herself higher in this book's ranking, but nothing has been beyond her means since she began her Group 1 harvest. Winter may not be over yet; that shiver you can feel is one of anticipation, not temperature.
STEVE DENNIS

## "That shiver you can feel is one of anticipation, not temperature"

# 50
## LADY REBECCA

Diminutive to look at she might have been, but Lady Rebecca was all heart and her insatiable desire to win made her one of the most enduring racemares in memory.

Her story stems from humble beginnings, but from little things big things did grow. As a yearling she was sold at Doncaster, only to be returned as a box-walker. With a blemish on her record, she sold for a second time 24 hours later to David Redvers for 400 guineas.

She was the first horse Redvers, now a well-respected bloodstock agent and racing manager to Qatar Racing, had bought at public auction and never will he make a more inspired purchase.

"She kick-started my career and that of Venetia Williams," Redvers says. "Having cost so little she was such a phenomenal Cinderella story and proved it's not the size of the cheque but the size of the heart that matters."

She was given time to mature at Tweenhills Farm before syndicated to the Kinnersley Optimists and joining Williams, in just her second season, after her first trainer Simon Christian retired. She hit the ground running.

"I used to ride her quite a bit and she moved like a greyhound – she was quite small but massively athletic," her trainer recalls.

Lady Rebecca rattled off three straight bumper wins for Williams, followed by two over hurdles, with her unbeaten run only ending at the 1998 Cheltenham Festival behind French Holly in the Royal & SunAlliance Novices' Hurdle.

That defeat proved merely a blip and her next three starts all ended with emphatic wins. By this time her record at Cheltenham was two wins from three runs and, with a proven penchant for Prest-

**Foaled**
Foaled May 11, 1992

**Pedigree**
Rolfe – Needwood
Fortune

**Breeder**
Needwood Stud

**Owners**
Kinnersley Optimists

**Trainer**
Venetia Williams

**Main jockey**
Norman Williamson

**Career record**
13 wins and three places
from 19 runs

**Most famous for**
Winning three
consecutive Cleeve
Hurdles

**Fate at stud**
Of five foals to run, two
have won, including
hat-trick scorer Lord
Generous. Her latest
runner is Lady Karina,
star of the *Racing Post*'s
*Born to Run* series

HAT-TRICK: Norman
Williamson holds three
fingers aloft after Lady
Rebecca completes a
Cleeve Hurdle treble in
2001 off the back off an
eight-month absence.
It was the last race of
a remarkable career

bury Park, her career never strayed far from her favourite track.

Between December 1998 and February 1999 Lady Rebecca rattled off a hat-trick of wins at Cheltenham by a combined winning margin of 45 lengths, including a 20-length romp in the Cleeve Hurdle.

That win made her a leading contender for the 1999 Stayers' Hurdle, where she cruised to the front after two out and remained in pole position until after the last. However, with the emphasis on stamina, she succumbed first to Le Coudray and then the fast-finishing winner Anzum with the post 100 yards away.

"The Cleeve was over two miles five, and at Cheltenham that was her distance," Williams says. "She led over the last in the Stayers' but didn't quite get home."

Normal service was resumed when she completed back-to-back Cleeve Hurdle wins following a ten-month absence, fighting tenaciously to hold off Bacchanal, who would take his revenge at the festival in March where Lady Rebecca was below her best.

She was also beaten at Punchestown on her next start, after which retirement and life as a broodmare beckoned, only for her to fail to get in foal and instead she returned to Williams for one last hurrah. Her crowning moment soon followed.

Expertly conditioned, Lady Rebecca made her return in the 2001 Cleeve, with a third straight win in the Grade 1 on the line.

Under regular rider Norman Williamson she made her move going down the hill, picked up the revs climbing up the other side and motored clear from the last for a decisive win that left Cheltenham tingling.

"The third Cleeve was special because she'd picked up an injury the previous season and had been retired," Williams says. "She was the most remarkable mare I've had anything to do with."

It proved a fitting finale as recurring foot problems meant she never raced again, ending her career as the winner of 13 of her 19 starts and with seven wins at her beloved Cheltenham.

After retiring to Redvers' Tweenhills Farm and Stud for her second career as a broodmare, Lady Rebecca died in 2013 at the age of 21 after suffering from colic.

"For all the thousands of horses I've had through my hands, I don't think there will be another who holds quite such a place," Redvers says.

**LEWIS PORTEOUS**

> "She was
> the most
> remarkable
> mare I've
> had anything
> to do with"